PORNOGRAPHY AND SEXUAL DEVIANCE

Pornography and Sexual Deviance

A Report of the Legal and Behavioral Institute
Beverly Hills, California

MICHAEL J. GOLDSTEIN

and

HAROLD SANFORD KANT

with JOHN J. HARTMAN

UNIVERSITY OF CALIFORNIA PRESS

BERKELEY · LOS ANGELES · LONDON

1973

University of California Press
Berkeley and Los Angeles, California
University of California Press, Ltd.
London, England
Copyright © 1973 by Michael Goldstein and
    Harold Sanford Kant
ISBN: 0-520-02406-0
Library of Congress Catalog Card Number: 72-97735
Designed by W. H. Snyder
Printed in the United States of America

6|76
6/86

CONTENTS

*We cannot expect or desire to
return to Greek morality, and its ideal
of "the beautiful alike in body and soul"
may be out of reach. But there can be little doubt
that we shall gradually break down
the false notions and the rigid attempts
at legal and social prohibitions
which have caused so much trouble
and confusion in the sexual history
of our recent past.*

HAVELOCK ELLIS

INTRODUCTION

This book is the report of a research program inspired by the need for scientifically obtained data on pornography and its effects. Necessarily included in such a study is the broader area of sexual conduct and sexual attitudes. Thus, the investigation must focus not only on erotic materials per se but also on the sexual histories of the persons selected for questioning.

A crucial issue of current social concern involves the possible link between pornography and the development of nonheterosexual or antisocial sexual behavior. Accordingly, the persons studied in this inquiry fall into four groups: a sample of those known to be extensive users of pornography; a sample of those whose sexual behavior is considered antisocial (convicted rapists and child-molesters); a sample including transsexuals seeking sex change operations, homosexuals, and lesbians; and a matched sample chosen from the general population.

The authors are not so presumptuous as to believe the present investigation shall be definitive. It developed as an extension of a pilot study supported by the U.S. Commission on Pornography and Obscenity, established in response to the apparently deep public concern about such materials. The extensive past efforts by the Institute of Sex Research of Indiana University (the "Kinsey Institute") served as a guide and checkpoint for our narrower approach.

Pornography is not a new subject for scientific examination. In 1929, the League of Nations established a commission called the "International Convention for the Suppression of the Circulation and Traffic in Obscene Publications." This group conducted a sociological investigation in selected member nations, and (as its name implies) was essentially concerned with finding ways to suppress material then considered obscene. The initial investigation was followed by numerous others

1

throughout the life of the League of Nations, and the trend continued during early years of the United Nations.

In 1960, the United States Congress established a "Commission on Noxious Printed and Pictured Material." The duties of the commission, as stated in the text of the bill establishing it, were to:

(1) conduct a scientific investigation of the relationship between the production, distribution, and sale, and reading or viewing of noxious printed or pictured material dealing with acts or suggestive acts of sexuality, and sexual deviations or perversions, and the commission by the readers or viewers thereof of criminal, delinquent, or other antisocial acts; and

(2) analyze the law pertaining thereto, and recommend appropriate revisions to the Congress.

One of the major conclusions stemming from this investigation was that Congress should encourage unprejudiced factual research performed by qualified scientists. In 1967, Congress responded by setting up another "Commission on Obscenity and Pornography," in a bill that included a mandate for such dispassionate broader research. The responsibilities of the 1967 Commission were as follows:

(1) with the aid of leading constitutional law authorities, to analyze the laws pertaining to the control of obscenity and pornography; and to evaluate and recommend definitions of obscenity and pornography;

(2) to ascertain the methods employed in the distribution of obscene and pornographic materials and to explore the nature and volume of traffic in such materials;

(3) to study the effect of obscenity and pornography upon the public, and particularly minors, and its relationship to crime and other antisocial behavior; and

(4) to recommend such legislative, administrative, or other advisable and appropriate action as the Commission deems necessary to regulate effectively the flow of such traffic, without in any way interfering with constitutional rights.

A significant portion of the data used in this book derives from the research we did for the 1967 Commission, and some of that information was included in the Commission's report. In this book, however, we have increased the subject population, made new analyses, and placed our findings in a broader frame of reference, allowing for greater scientific and public scrutiny and debate. In the process, we have tried to avoid the moral and religious bias that has colored polemical writings on this subject, and to concentrate specifically on those issues confronting the Commission.

In previous interview studies, such as those carried on at the Kinsey

Institute, pornography has been examined only as a secondary issue in the larger context of sexual deviation, and experimental studies of pornographic stimuli have been limited by the range of groups studied. Thus, most research to date has produced scattered and inconclusive pieces of information — evidence from which it has been difficult to generalize. Our research, by contrast, is directly concerned with the psychological effects of pornography.

In the evaluative sections of this work, we endeavor, by bringing together principles of psychology and law, to generate public discussion and further research, and to impart a new perspective on the pornography issue to the people responsible for legislative decision-making. We do not concern ourselves with the possible "moral" implications of the use or production of pornography. Our basic question is whether or not the use of pornography is injurious to society. Does it present some clear and present danger that should be averted? Does it lead to antisocial behavior, including sexual assaults by one person against another? Does it encourage sexual aberrations that society, at present, believes it has an interest in preventing even though no criminal behavior is involved? Is Justice William Rehnquist correct when he assumes, in his opinion in *California v. LaRue,* 409 U.S. 109 (1972), that indecent exposure and sexual assaults result from adult males viewing nude female ladies and certain sex acts in California bars? Or, might there conceivably be value to society in the availability of pornographic materials and entertainment — and, if so, does it outweigh or sufficiently offset any negative considerations?

Thus far, we have used the term "pornography" without definition. Research in dictionaries, encyclopedias, and other scholarly studies, as well as in court cases, produces little agreement. These disparate views, however, contribute much toward a fuller understanding of the subject, and we have devoted chapter 1 to a discussion of the various approaches to defining obscenity and pornography. This report points up the major problems society has traced to pornography, the range of positions taken on the issue, and the significance of past analyses for our research. It also indicates the necessity for a practical operational definition of pornography for purposes of research, one that is readily understandable and based on common sense. In our view, the content analysis approach (see chap. 1), though by no means infallible, best satisfies these criteria.

Chapter 2 reviews previous research relevant to our study. Chapter 3 discusses the logic and development of the questionnaire (interview instrument) used in our research. Chapter 4 defines the groups studied, elaborates on our selection process, and compares the groups from a socioeconomic standpoint.

Chapter 5 reports on the frequency of exposure to pornography during various periods of the subjects' lives, including preadolescence, adolescence, and maturity, and makes cross-comparisons between the different study groups. Chapter 6 and 7 examine those experiences with pornography that each subject selected as the most important for him in each of those periods. Chapters 8 and 9 contain a more detailed analysis of the subjects' recent experiences with pornography.

Chapter 10 is concerned with the connection between sex fantasies and pornography, and an analysis of the role of fantasy in sexual behavior.

In chapter 11, the sex attitudes and practices of the subjects are summarized and analyzed with regard to the data on exposure to pornography, followed by a discussion of the implications for further research.

Chapter 12 deals with the legal and political issues involved in the censorship of pornography, and relates our findings to the legal process.

In any study of this kind, many people have made significant contributions. We are particularly grateful to W. Cody Wilson, Staff Director of the United States Commission on Obscenity and Pornography, for support and advice; to Lewis King, Ph.D., who served as Project Director and consultant in writing this report; and to Virginia Shabaik, who kept us organized and coherent. Lewis L. Judd, M.D. and Richard Green, M.D. (Director of the Gender Identity Clinic, UCLA) were of great help in designing the study and providing cases. Paul Bramwell, Ph.D. and Frank Vanasek, Ph.D., of Atascadero State Hospital, were essential in locating the sex offender sample, in training the interviewers for that sample, and in many other helpful ways. Dorr Legg, president of One Incorporated, was of great assistance in supporting this research with his membership and in locating homosexual respondents. Whatever verve and life exists in the prose of this book is very much due to the efforts of Susan Moscov and Jennifer Alkire who insisted that we translate everything into English! Special thanks are due Janet Goldstein, Eleanor Walker, and Shirley Warren for their kind assistance in the preparation of the manuscript.

*Pornography is one of the most
restricted of the literary arts,
I was even about to say
one of the purest.*

CLIFTON FADIMAN

*Pornography is a cancer of society;
it must be excised from the body politic
if the nation is to survive
with wholesome vigor.*

RICHARD KYLE-KEITH

1

WHAT IS PORNOGRAPHY?

Throughout history, in pictures and in words, man has recorded his preoccupation with the sexual side of his nature. From carvings in the ancient Hindu temples of Kahjurah to the murals uncovered in the ruins of Pompeii, from bawdy Boccaccio to erotic violence in the de Sade, man's sexuality continually asserts itself. Confronted with this vivid evidence of irrepressible sexual energy, almost every age and every culture has chosen to impose its own limits, regulating human sexual behavior and its visual portrayal, through ritual, religion, or law. Many ancient peoples reserved a special season of the year as a time to throw aside the customary restraints of law and morality, give themselves up to extravagant mirth and jollity, and find a vent for their darker passions which would never be allowed them in the more staid and sober course of ordinary life. The Roman Empire's cult of Dionysius and feast of Saturn exemplify sanctioned sexuality, regulated by ritual as to time, place, and duration. Some of these practices, reshaped to blend with early Christian ritual, served to reinforce the precept that salvation required the suppression rather than celebration of carnal pleasures. Sex linked man to the devil and was therefore to be cast out. The phallus, once a sacred symbol of fertility, came to be viewed as a thorn in the flesh.

Although organized religion dangled eternal salvation as the reward for chastity outside the sanctity of marriage and celibacy in the priest-hood, the bait was not particularly effective. Unregenerate monks still composed bawdy songs. Calvin's energetic sermons did not banish prostitution from Western Europe. And theatrical performances, despite intermittent censorship, enthusiastically contrasted the pleasures of swearing, drinking, and whoring with the drawbacks of conventional marriage.

During the first half of the nineteenth century, the stronghold of religion, especially in England and America, was invaded and irreparably damaged by research in every area then open to scientific study. Darwin's *Origin of Species* forced men to reevaluate their role in the universe, and eventually to accept themselves as a culmination of animal evolution. The establishment of new social sciences — anthropology, sociology, and psychology — contributed to a world view that was increasingly secular. Intellectually, men "traveled from the phantasies of the book of Genesis to a knowledge of geology; . . . from the conception of special creation out of nothing, to the doctrine of development" (Schroeder, 1954). As a corollary to the loosened bonds of religious dogma and the expanded perception of scientific thought, more detailed and realistic physical depiction of sexuality in art and letters was inevitable. The benefits to the printing industry from improved machine technology were ample. Publishing as a mass medium dates from this time. Lending libraries, daily newspapers, and cheap magazines served a large and voracious reading public. Naturally, the production of lewd books kept pace with the output of more pristine titles.

The portrayal of sex in all media continues to increase exponentially. Books that had to be smuggled into the country ten years ago are now available in most public libraries, and films that formerly were seen only at stag shows now play at the neighborhood movie theater. Many parents, educators, and clergymen have become alarmed; they fear that this increasing exposure to erotic materials will twist young minds, encouraging depravity and sex crimes. Their concern has led to an increasing utilization of the court system to define the criteria for *legally* sanctioned erotic art, as distinguished from *illegal* pornography.

The legal ramifications of the pornography issue are examined in detail in chapter 12, but the fundamental dilemma is obvious: the courts are influenced in large part by community attitudes in evaluating the propriety of erotic materials, and the community forms its attitudes on the basis of those materials the courts approve for public consumption.

As one consequence of this statement, defense counsel in pornography cases now tend to maneuver for the longest possible delay in bringing cases to trial. Their hope is that continued public exposure to the material in question will result in "liberalized" community standards and attitudes, increasing the chances for acquittal of their clients. Since legal restraints on prior censorship permit the defendants to continue to sell and exhibit their wares pending trial, they can act to change the relevant tests of legality (encompassing community standards of acceptability and practice) even while they are awaiting trial.

DOES PORNOGRAPHY SERVE A FUNCTIONAL ROLE IN SOCIETY?

Social scientists, observing the difficulties courts have encountered with the issue of pornography, have tried to suggest new approaches. Influenced and perhaps enlightened by their exposure to anthropological and psychological research, some social scientists are willing to regard pornography as an acceptable element of our culture. They assume that pornography serves some necessary function, that it may help to ameliorate some pressing social problem.

The Kronhausens (1964) attempted to distinguish between artistic erotica and pornography in terms of its content. Their functional analysis antedated a more systematic one by Polsky (1967), who argues that:

Prostitution and pornography occur in every society large enough to have a reasonably complex division of labor; and although pornography develops only in a rudimentary way in preliterate societies (by means of erotic folk tales and simple pictorial or sculptural devices) whenever a society has a fair degree of literacy and mass communication technology then pornography becomes a major functional alternative to prostitution.

In accordance with this functional view of the role of erotica, the Kronhausens attempted to use content analysis to provide a set of criteria to distinguish *pornography* from *erotically realistic art* or *fiction.* Their analysis of various erotic works led them to conclude that the primary aim of pornography is to arouse the viewer or reader by portraying sexual relations in which all conventional standards are violated and the only psychological feelings involved are lust and relief of sexual tensions. More serious works, on the other hand, attempt to depict the broad spectrum of human emotions typical of such intimate relationships. Thus, the Kronhausens point out, we see in pornography repetitive seduction themes involving a "victim" who is in fact a willing collaborator, rape or defloration in which little concern for the victim's pain or resentment is expressed, and a generally exploitative view of human relationships.

In short, while erotically realistic work may be just as graphic as pornography in its description of sexual intercourse and deviance, it also acknowledges the complexities of the feelings involved (such as fear, guilt, ambivalence, disgust, etc.) and presents the central figures as human beings rather than as sexual animals. Thus the Kronhausens discriminate between pornography and erotically realistic fiction on the basis of the general view of man expressed in the work, not the explicitness with which sexual relations are described.

The philosopher Abraham Kaplan (1955), while sympathetic to the need for distinct definitions of pornography and erotic art, felt that the two categories proposed by the Kronhausens were not sufficient, and suggested four instead. His first category, *conventional obscenity*, includes material that "attacks established sexual patterns and practices." Zola, Ibsen, and Shaw exemplify the degree of unconventionality measured here. All attacked the flagrant economic, political, and social injustices of their day. Shaw's play, *Mrs. Warren's Profession,* while hardly a manual for a career in prostitution, shocked Victorian society because it dared to examine and question traditional and tacit assumptions about the role of the sexes. The second category, *Dionysian obscenity,* is characterized by "excessive sexualism" that celebrates man's unity with nature. Sex is a joyous revel, "a symbolic release of impulses thwarted in fact." *Fanny Hill* and *Lady Chatterly's Lover* propagandize beautiful sex gracefully and happily performed. The "yes" motif from Molly Bloom's famous concluding soliloquy in *Ulysses* affirms man's sexuality as part of his wholeness. The third category, *perverse obscenity,* presents sex as dirty, fearful, and secretive. Many writers have stressed the shameful pleasure that scores of schoolmasters once derived from beating and bullying their students. Until recent years the depiction of homosexual love would have belonged in this category. Now, largely through the dedicated efforts of homosexual writers and the receptivity of more enlightened readers, such literature is rated less harmful. The fourth category, *pornography of violence,* depicts "sexual desires . . . transformed into acts of aggression." Magazines and paperbacks in which the heroes would rather kill than kiss, mail-order sales of boots and whips, all attest to a large if furtive audience for this hardest core of the pornographic hierarchy.

LIMITATIONS OF THE CONTENT ANALYSIS APPROACH

Labeling pornographic content as a means of separating "good" erotic writing from "bad" pornography is, however, ultimately self-defeating: those who must interpret and somehow implement the descriptive categories through prohibitions on printing and sales are themselves controlled by subjective considerations. Defining pornography through textual analysis without some kind of factual common reference point is as futile as were the efforts of medieval scholars to define "nature" without looking out the window. Until the Kinsey report, few studies by social scientists had dealt with the realities of human sexual behavior, and none could serve as guides for establishing such reference points for an analysis of erotica.

It is easy to understand the scientists' hesitancy to undertake such studies. We have come a great distance in permissiveness and toleration about sexual matters. Things are more open and ventilated. But there is a residue of resistance and fear, a notion that research into sexual matters is somehow disreputable. Kinsey courageously withstood severe criticism from both the academic community and the general public during his pioneering years, because he was convinced that no part of our material universe, especially "the more complex behavior of the human," should be exempt from scientific scrutiny. We are indebted to him as much for his methods as for the results he obtained. Kinsey's systematic approach — sampling, questionnaires, intensive interviews, evaluations, all recognized tools of the modern scientific investigator — enabled him to measure and record actual sexual practices and habits in America. His conclusions, based on the data thus obtained, constituted proven facts rather than casual speculations. Kinsey authenticated the infinite variety of American sexual attitudes and practices, a discovery that belied the middle-class man's claim to semi-Victorian habits. His research methods and his results shattered our traditional notions of appropriate sexual patterns, including those involving symbolic portrayals of sexuality, for his data presented objective evidence concerning the many diverse stimuli that his respondents found sexually arousing.

MODELING AND CATHARSIS THEORIES ON THE IMPACT OF EROTICA

To the Greeks, *pornographos* meant "writing of harlots." In a sense modern society has revived this ancient connotation with its insistence that pornographic art represents a kind of social disease, a potential danger to personal and national health. Hence, the current demand for some consistent form of censorship.

All censorship relies on a content analysis of the material in question, designed to assess (a) the intent of the creator and (b) the probable effects of exposure to the material on the behavior of the reader or viewer. When the late J. Edgar Hoover stated that "pornography is a major cause of sex violence," he was relying on the "modeling" theory:

the notion that behavior as portrayed in books, pictures, or films is contagious. (Obviously, the theory applies to praiseworthy as well as undesirable behavior.)

Speculation on both aspects of censorship has proliferated in judicial attempts to define legal criteria for obscenity. The courts, however, have had to operate without factual evidence regarding the second aspect, the effects of pornography on sexual behavior, although at times it has been assumed that pornography represents a dangerous influence. See, for example, the majority opinion of Justice Rehnquist in *California v. LaRue,* 409 U.S. 109 (1972), discussed in chapter 12. This book is concerned with precisely this issue. Does a chaste individual become a fornicator after reading pornography? Does a marriage constricted by sexual inhibitions become freer as a result of exposure to simulated intercourse in a theater? And if indeed the marriage benefits, can we accept a more positive role for the pornographic stimulus? It seems just as plausible that a sex education course or manual might serve pornographic purposes as that pornography might assist in the sex education process. Do erotic books and films lower sexual tensions through producing an emotional release, or do they increase them through heightened awareness on the part of the spectators?

The ultimate question is whether obscene and pornographic works serve as models for imitation, leading to acts of violence and encouraging perverted or unconventional sexual behavior; or whether they actually help to prevent such acts through the release of sexual tension (catharsis). In undertaking the research we report on here, we hoped to examine these questions in an empirical framework, through methodical analysis of the impact of erotica on the lives of convicted sex offenders and members of nonheterosexual groups, as well as persons from the general community with no identifiably unorthodox sexual proclivities. In this work we review the literature on the behavioral effects of erotic stimuli, and then present data and conclusions derived from our own study (developed for the U.S. Commission on Pornography and Obscenity) of the long-term effects of exposure to erotic materials on various groups.

In discussing this research, we focus upon: (1) the frequency of exposure to erotic stimuli in the formative preadolescent and adolescent years; (2) the special impact that the most vivid adolescent experience with erotica may have had upon sexual attitudes and behavior; (3) the frequency of exposure to erotica during a recent adult period, the year prior to the study; (4) a comparable survey of the most vivid experience with erotica during that previous year; and (5) the relationship between an individual's sexual daydreams or fantasies and his reactions to erotica.

Through an analysis of this data, we hope to begin to reveal whether antisocial and nonheterosexual sex behavior is associated with the degree of an individual's exposure to erotica during the formative years. In addition, we hope to establish the impact, if any, of certain especially vivid memories of erotica, the "peak experience," on sexual attitudes and behavior. Do these peak experiences stimulate sexual experimentation during adolescence? During adulthood? What impact do they have upon sexual value systems — for example, the archetypal views of man-woman relationships which we carry into our adult lives. Do our sex fantasies grow out of erotica, or do we search out erotica that matches our preexisting fantasies? In general, can we say that serious deviations in sexual behavior are correlated with the type or frequency of exposure to erotic stimuli, or the age at which exposure occurs? Can we conclude that pornography represents a clear and present danger to our social organization, justifying governmental censorship over the production and distribution of these materials?

We shall address ourselves to each of these issues in various chapters of this book. We hope that the evidence presented may assist legislators and public officials to deal with the pornography question in a rational manner.

*The Franciscan friar whom I meet
on the mountain trail in Peru looks at me
in puzzlement for a time and then says,
"Ah, es el Señor Doctor Kinsey, no?" Then, he wants to know
why we are doing this research and when I reply,
"Porque, padre, es una parte de la vida"
— because, father, it is part of life — he instantly responds,
"Si, es una parte de la vida" and for the rest
of the mountain journey we
are good friends.*

ALFRED C. KINSEY

2

REVIEW OF LITERATURE ON EFFECTS
OF PORNOGRAPHY

As we indicated in chapter 1, from Kinsey's practical approach to the investigation of sexual behavior springs our motive and our method. But what additions have other scientists contributed to this original fund of knowledge in the past thirty years? In this chapter we will survey the existing literature as it relates to our study of reactions to pornography.

Generally, the scientific literature on the effects of exposure to pornographic stimuli is sparse indeed. Often we found ourselves reviewing literature on the effects of exposure to erotic stimuli that bore little if any resemblance to pornography (e.g., pictures of films that suggested nudity or sexual relations only indirectly). Often we had to extrapolate broadly to draw inferences from research oriented to very different issues. Yet certain consistencies emerged in our review that proved helpful in the design of our own research.

In understanding the effects of pornography on behavior, we must distinguish between immediate and long-term effects. The immediate effects can be emotional reactions to the stimulus, such as sexual arousal, disgust, or anger. Also, erotic stimuli may instantly elicit sexual fantasies — perhaps identical with others previously experienced, or new ones stemming from the particular stimulus in question. The fantasies may be brief and transitory or they may persist longer and recur periodically like movie flashbacks. A third immediate response to an erotic stimulus can be overt sexual behavior. The reader or viewer, in reaction to the material, masturbates, approaches some available sex partner, or — in the view of thinkers like Justice Rehnquist — turns to an unwilling sex partner for relief of sexual tension. The sexual arousal, if it occurs, may lead to imitation of behavior represented in the pornographic stimulus or may merely activate previously established patterns of sexual behavior.

These immediate reactions to erotica can be distinguished from more long-range effects. Exposure to erotica at a particular age may shape an individual's sexual attitudes and values, although the results of this shaping process will not be evident until much later. Part of the social concern regarding pornography derives from the fear that young children or adolescents may be adversely affected in maturity by early contact with pornographic materials. For example, Bandura and his associates (1961), in their research on the imitation of aggression, have suggested that children can learn and suppress antisocial behavior patterns which may then surface at a later time when a facilitating environment is present.

These long-term effects of pornography are of vital concern. Yet almost all the research to date has dealt only with short-term effects. The few investigations concerned with long-term effects are retrospective interview studies, such as those carried out by Kinsey and his colleagues (1948, 1953). This review will focus first on articles dealing with the immediate effects, and then summarize the few concerned with long-term effects. We will consider several different variables: the stimulus itself, the social context of the exposure, the subject's emotional temperament, and the subject's sexual experience and experience with erotica.

IMMEDIATE EFFECTS OF PORNOGRAPHY

THE PORNOGRAPHIC STIMULUS

It has long been recognized that erotic stimuli include a wide range of subjects, from partial nudity to explicit portrayals of unrestrained sexual relations. The media of presentation also varies, from line drawings to full-color movies to live entertainment. Given these differing degrees of naturalism, it seems plausible that stimuli would vary in their immediate arousal value.

The earliest evidence that responses are dependent upon the content of the erotic stimulus comes from the large-scale interview study carried out by Kinsey (1948). In the course of interviewing respondents about their sexual behavior, Kinsey asked about reactions to erotica. A sizable proportion of the sample, both male and female, reported that they experienced sexual arousal from material portraying nudity or sexual acts. They also rated the various materials according to the likelihood of arousal. The impact of these materials differed for males and females, a point we discuss below. If one examines the Kinsey data for males (see table 1), it is evident that the level of response to stimuli depends on the degree of realism involved.

If we examine the *definitely frequent* category, males report that actual observance of sex acts is the most powerful stimulus. Next are burlesques or floor shows, and least arousing are commercial films. For the males in this sample, the more direct and unambiguous the sexual cue, the more likely it is that arousal will occur. (Kinsey's data, of course, are based on reactions prior to revision of the film rating code. It is conceivable that, in this era of the "X"-rated film, commercial films

Table 1

FREQUENCY OF SEXUAL RESPONSES TO DIFFERENT EROTIC
STIMULI REPORTED BY MALES IN KINSEY STUDY

	Sexual Arousal Response			
Stimuli	*Definitely Frequent (%)*	*Sometimes (%)*	*Never (%)*	*Size of Sample*
Portrayals of nudes	18	36	46	4191
Observing genitalia	"Many"	"Many"	"Few"	617
Commercial films	6	30	64	3231
Burlesques	28	34	38	3377
Observing sex acts	42	35	23	3868
Reading* romantic material	21	38	41	3952
Reading* erotic stories	16	31	53	4202

* In this study, Kinsey distinguished between commercially available romantic literature and erotic literature available through illicit sources. This distinction makes little sense in the United States today.

would not be rated as low in arousal value as they were in the 1940s.)

It is worth noting that Kinsey's ratings were derived from interviews with adults. Whether adolescents are aroused by the same sexual cues is not so clear. The study by Ramsey (1943) presents some indirect evidence on this matter. He interviewed 280 boys in early (eleven to fourteen) and late (fifteen to eighteen) adolescence and administered questionnaires on their sexual development. He asked his respondents to rank fifteen potentially erotic stimuli on a scale of arousal potential. He found that the younger adolescent group ranked the following three experiences as having the highest arousal value: conversation about sex, female nudity, and obscene pictures (type not specified). For older adolescents, the most arousing stimuli were female nudity, daydreaming, and obscene pictures. The only age trend noted in the Ramsey data was that internal cognitive cues (daydreaming) become more important to men as they grow older.

If we place the Kinsey and Ramsey data together, they suggest that prior sexual experience affects reactions to erotica. With greater sexual experience, more direct representations of sexual activity are found to be arousing. Even daydreaming requires some sexual experience to form its core content, and thus will probably not occur before late adolescence.

Levitt (1969) has attempted to scale the sexual arousal value of stimuli in a more systematic fashion, asking subjects to rate the arousal value of photos and drawings depicting varieties of sexual objects and activities. His raters were a very narrowly based sample, consisting of male graduate students at a university. Given Kinsey's numerous findings of sharp differences in sexual practices and attitudes as a function of social status (of which educational level is one important determinant factor) one cannot overgeneralize from Levitt's data. Still, they are worth examining for interesting leads.

Levitt asked his subjects to rate nineteen sexual themes represented in photographs. The results are illustrated in table 2. He found that the order of these ratings remained consistent when a subject repeated his ratings at another time and when different subjects rated the same stimuli — even when different sets of photos were submitted to the subjects. We can see in table 2 that pictures of heterosexual intercourse, heterosexual petting, and heterosexual fellatio are ranked 1 to 5 respectively in arousal value. Surprisingly, a photo of a nude female alone, performing no sexual activity, ranks 6 in arousal value over such "hardcore" stimuli as the group sex picture or the nude female masturbating. This ranking is particularly interesting as the females were evidently professional models who posed in totally unsuggestive positions.

Another surprise in Levitt's data is the relatively high arousal rating

Table 2

RANK ORDERING OF SEXUAL AROUSAL PROPERTIES
BY A GROUP OF MALE GRADUATE STUDENTS
(Levitt and Hinesley, 1969)

1. Heterosexual coitus in the ventral-ventral position
2. Heterosexual coitus in the ventral-dorsal position
3. Heterosexual petting, participants nude
4. Heterosexual petting, participants partly-clad
5. Heterosexual fellatio
6. Nude female
7. Heterosexual cunnilingus
8. Masturbation by a female
9. A triad of two females and one male in conjunctive behavior involving coitus and oral-genital activity
10. Partly-clad female
11. Homosexual cunnilingus
12. Homosexual petting by females
13. Sadomasochistic behavior, male on female
14. Homosexual fellatio
15. Sadomasochistic behavior, female on male
16. Masturbation by a male
17. Homosexual anal coitus
18. Nude male
19. Partly-clad male

accorded the photos of the partially nude female. These pictures were relatively innocuous: one displayed no more than bare thighs above stocking tops; a second was a rather standard pose in lingerie; and a third portrayed a fully clad woman seated on the ground in such a way as to appear to accidentally expose her panties. This suggests that nudity itself and other contextual factors in a stimulus — the intent of the photo, its artistry, and like factors — may be as important in determining the response as the activity represented.

The significance of nudity as an erotic cue had been explored previously by Levitt and Hinesley (1967) in a study in which two sets of photos portraying similar sexual activity were presented to subjects. In one set, the participants were fully nude; in the other, they were partially nude with only genitals shown. Raters reported 38 percent more sexual arousal from the nude set than from the partially nude set.

Despite these suggestions that nudity makes a significant contribution to sexual arousal in an erotic stimulus, Levitt's data does support the

Kinsey data in one important sense. The more explicit the representation of heterosexual intercourse, the higher the rated sexual arousal.

While numerous writers have intimated the importance of the broader context surrounding an erotic stimulus, there are few studies dealing with this problem. Levitt's study suggests that the intent of the stimulus as perceived by the viewer is significant. An "accidental" view of underpants is more erotic than a stimulus clearly designed to arouse, such as a female masturbating. But are films designed purely to arouse, such as stag movies, more or less arousing than general distribution films that portray similar sexual activity within the context of a story that permits identification with the characters? When the film maker's intent is aesthetic, the specific scenes portraying sexual activity are directly linked to the buildup of general tension and involvement. The potential for sexual arousal inherent in this treatment of erotic scenes represents a fertile area of investigation.

Jakobovits (1965) attempted to study this type of variable in written portrayals of sexual activity. Following the Kronhausens (1964), he defined two types of stories: *erotic realism,* designed for a realistic portrayal of sexual activity, as opposed to *hard-core pornography,* based on wish-fulfilling distortions of "normal" sexuality. While Jakobovits's data relate to differences in arousal stimuli for males and females, his study is interesting as an attempt to define a dimension of reality-fantasy in the form and content of literary erotic scenes. Unfortunately, his study does not deal with this dimension in a systematic fashion. It would be useful to know whether written descriptions of sexual activity the reader has previously experienced are as arousing as descriptions of erotic activities rarely if ever experienced. This fantasy-reality dimension is significant as a means of determining how identification with or dissociation from the characters in an erotic stimulus contributes to the arousal value of that stimulus.

Modern-day commercial pornography depends increasingly on the fantasy context. Witness these ads from a Danish firm describing the subject matter of color photo magazines available: "Two nuns are raped by a drunk sailor and the two pious women are changed to foaming vampires." "The teacher seduces two quite young school girls, but the girls are willing tools in his eager hands." "Two lesbian girls are disturbed in their game by a lecherous young man and together those three meet with their greatest orgasm." The fantasy-reality dimension obviously relates to the media of presentation. Photos are more likely to be realistic while media that lend themselves to fantasy, such as books and films, can show some variance on this continuum.

A look at a few fantasies commonly portrayed in commercial pornography enables us to make an educated guess concerning stimuli likely to be arousing. Certain themes appear rather frequently, among them the release of sexuality in the innocent (or repressed) and helpless female by the potent male. With his aid, her animal nature is exposed, and immediately she craves sex with the hunger of an addict.

In the best-selling manual *The Sensuous Woman* (by the anonymous "J"), the female author describes recurring sexual fantasies reported to her by her lovers (pp. 152–155), including the one mentioned above:

Fantasy Number Two: A gorgeous unknown female is chained to the wall. He [the man having the fantasy] begins to do very erotic things to her while she writhes in helpless resistance. Slowly, thanks to his superb technique . . . she begins to respond to him and then goes crazy with passion. Slowly he unchains her and she throws herself upon him and makes love to *him*.

This fantasy of the potent male releasing the female's repressed sexuality occurs with such frequency in erotic literature that it might be considered an archetype, in the Jungian sense.

Also common is the passive male fantasy, described by "J" as follows:

Fantasy Number Three: At least two and sometimes three, four, five or even six women of various hues and shapes all make love to the fantasizer at once. Sometimes this takes place at an orgy. Other times they are alone.

Fantasy Number Four: He lies there helpless to resist while this enchanting vision of female sexuality forces herself upon him, finally completely possessing him.

While "J's" list of fantasies is hardly the result of systematic research, it does coincide closely with those that occur in written and filmed pornography. It seems probable that a few elemental themes recur in all stories or films, suggesting that these themes have particularly strong arousal value. Why should it be that in our culture the transition of the innocent or unwilling female into a sex addict is apparently so exciting? Do we still harken to the puritan myth that women should not enjoy sexuality, and that any attempt to arouse them is tantamount to corrupting innocent souls? Or do we see a variation on the myth of Eve, the original temptress, tamed by men after the fiasco of Eden, still capable of a return to intense sexuality?

A recent survey of *Playboy* magazine readers (*Playboy,* February 1973, p. 121), carried out by two of the authors (Michael J. Goldstein and Harold S. Kant) dealt with the varieties of sex fantasies experienced. The survey results indicated that, indeed, a small number of highly popular sex fantasies, very similar in content to the basic themes of erotica, recurred in the minds of these readers. The variations in these themes reflect certain underlying parameters that are valid for the systematic analysis of both self-generated fantasies and commercial erotica. They are: (1) the variety of sexual activities portrayed; (2) the activity or passivity of the central character or hero; (3) the reality or fantasy nature of the hero's sex partner; and (4) the exotic or conventional nature of the sexual activities described.

THE CONTEXT OF EXPOSURE TO AN EROTIC STIMULUS

Our reactions to any stimulus depend upon the situation in which it occurs, including the elements of place (at home or in public); other people present (and their relationship to us); and other social factors that influence our expressions of feelings or behavior. There are not many studies that bear directly on the context of erotic stimuli, but a few suggest indirectly that reactions to erotica depend upon the social context of exposure.

The study most frequently cited is one by Clark (1952), orginally designed to examine the effects of sexual arousal by an erotic stimulus on subsequent sexual fantasy. Clark hypothesized that exposure to photos of nudes would increase a subject's tendency to experience sexual fantasies when shown a standard picture from a projective test, the Thematic Apperception Test (TAT). He further suggested that the subjects would describe their fantasies more freely if they were measured in a permissive, guilt-free situation. Clark also expected that greater sexual arousal would occur when the subjects were intoxicated. Unfortunately, in Clark's study the manipulation of the social context and the sober-drunk factors were linked to one another, which makes interpretation of his results difficult.

Clark presented nude pictures to male subjects in one of two situations: (1) a group-testing situation in a university classroom, and (2) a fraternity beer party. After the subjects had been exposed to photos of nude females by one experimenter, a second administered a group session of the TAT which required subjects to create short stories based on eight relatively ambiguous pictures of interpersonal scenes. When the stories (similar to fantasy productions) were scored for the presence or absence of sexual content, Clark found more sexual content in the stories obtained in the party situation than in those obtained in the university classroom. Ironically, in the classroom situation there were fewer stories containing sexual themes following exposure to nude photos than when subjects had been preexposed to neutral nonsexual pictures. The classroom situation actively inhibited the verbalization of sexual fantasy stories above the baseline of this control group. The increase in sexual themes in the fraternity party condition is more difficult to interpret, as it may have reflected the uninhibiting effects of alcohol, the party atmosphere, or some combination of causes.

Another study by Mussen and Scodel (1955) indicates more clearly the effects of the social context on sexual fantasy expression. They followed a procedure very similar to that of Clark but varied the formality of the laboratory situation in which the sexual arousal stimuli were presented. Male college students were shown pictures of nude females and instructed to rate each picture on a dimension of attractiveness. The slides were presented to one group by a formal, professional, and somewhat stern man in his sixties. A young, informal, relaxed graduate student administered the same slides to a second group. As soon as subjects had rated the nude pictures, TAT cards were administered to all of them by a third experimenter. The results showed that the group with the graduate student produced more thematic stories containing sexual themes than did the group with the older, more formal experimenter. These results were interpreted as indicating that the atmosphere of disapproval generated by the more authoritative and formal experimenter led to inhibition of sexual fantasy expression.

While these studies are hardly conclusive, they do suggest that the situation of exposure plays a significant role in the subsequent verbalization of sexual fantasies. Whether equal arousal of sexual desire occurs in different situational contexts, though verbalization of sexual thoughts may be inhibited, or whether the total sequence of arousal-verbalization is inhibited, remains an unsolved issue.

One factor not investigated is the potentially stimulating effect of a taboo social context. For example, the experience of viewing erotica in forbidden social contexts (church, classroom) may actually facilitate sexual arousal, while at the same time inhibiting overt expression of this arousal. This more complex contextual pattern clearly needs closer study, as the stimulating value of "forbidden fruit" undoubtedly plays a significant role in the arousal value of pornography. Where no rules prohibit the viewing of nudity or sexual material, is the likelihood of arousal increased or decreased?

In the two studies quoted above, the dependent variable was verbalization of a story containing sexual themes. There is little evidence concerning the facilitation or inhibition of overt sexual behavior by the situation of exposure to erotic material. The assumption is that if fantasy is inhibited, surely overt sexual behavior would be also. Research on aggression has indicated, however, that a direct correlation between fantasy expression of aggression and overt aggressive behavior is by no means inevitable (Staub and Konn, 1970). Very aggressive people frequently produce aggressive fantasy stories, but similar stories may also be offered by nonaggressive people. In this research, the issue of inner controls or guilt reappears again and again as a significant factor. Aggressive fantasy stories that indicate anxiety about punishment predict low overt aggression. As an analogy, situations that elicit guilt or anxiety about the expression of sexuality may inhibit the sexual fantasy from culminating in some overt sexual behavior. Sexual arousal by erotic stimuli may be a significant activator of sexual fantasies, but the verbal or active expression of these fantasies is partly a function of the situation.

In our research, we have used intensive interview questioning as a means of identifying the context of exposure to erotic stimuli and determining how this context facilitates or inhibits subsequent sexual behavior. This kind of detailed questioning represents a first step in isolating specific variables requiring closer experimental study.

The Person. By and large, the greatest bulk of research on the effects of pornography has focused on the person who is exposed to it. Every stimulus exists to some extent in the "eye of the beholder," who gives it meaning and significance. There is an old story about the patient who, after completing the Rorschach inkblot test, castigated the psychologist for showing him so many "dirty" pictures. In one sense, a pornographic stimulus can be defined objectively in terms of the objects and activities represented, but in another sense, these objective characteristics are given meaning only through a viewer's perceptual filters. In the rest of this chapter, we focus on those individual differences that account for people's varying reactions to erotica. These differences reflect both an individual's social learning regarding sex, and his impulse control in general. For at least one factor, the sex of the pornography user, it is difficult to determine whether we are dealing with issues of inborn temperament or the subtle effects of sex role training.

Sex (Male-Female) Differences in Response to Erotica. We indicated above, in reproducing a table from Kinsey (table 1), that we were presenting the data for males only. Table 3 illustrates the results of Kinsey's research on arousal value of different stimuli with regard to females.

A cursory glance at both tables points up the marked differences between male and female responses, though a substantial number of females and males report arousal by observing genitals. Females report greater arousal from seeing commercial films or reading materials in which sexuality is embedded in a romantic context. The more direct and explicit expressions of sexuality, arousing to males, have less influence on females, according to the Kinsey data. (This statistic, however, may

Table 3

FREQUENCY OF SEXUAL RESPONSES TO DIFFERENT EROTIC
STIMULI REPORTED BY FEMALES IN KINSEY STUDY

Stimuli	Sexual Arousal Response			Size of Sample
	Definitely Frequent (%)	*Sometimes* (%)	*Never* (%)	
Portrayals of nudes	3	9	88	5698
Observing genitalia	21	27	52	617
Commercial films	9	39	52	5411
Burlesques	4	10	86	2550
Observing sex acts	14	18	68	2242
Reading romantic material	16	44	40	5691
Reading erotic stories	2	12	86	5523

in part reflect the state of our culture at the time of Kinsey's investigation.)

There are indications that, within a female population, those who report more masculine interests and values respond more emphatically to erotic stimuli. Loiselle and Mollenauer (1965) investigated the physiological responsiveness (Palmar skin resistance changes) of two groups of females chosen on the basis of their scores on the Masculinity-Femininity (Mf) scale of the Minnesota Multiphasic Personality Inventory (MMPI). Twenty female subjects were used, ten who rated at the high (masculine) end of the scale and ten who rated at the low (feminine) end. The skin resistance responses of the women were recorded while they viewed eighteen projected color pictures (nine male and nine female in three poses and three degrees of undress — clothed, semiclothed, and nude). Results of this test showed that *all* the women reacted more strongly to male pictures than to female pictures, but the ten subjects with greater masculine tendencies had a significant reaction to *all* the pictures representing some degree of nudity. In other words, women who resemble men to some extent in their interests and values will probably respond, like men, to all kinds of erotic photos.

The 1965 study by Jakobovits discussed earlier appears, on the surface, to contradict the distinction projected by Loiselle and Mollenaur. In his investigation of male and female reactions to two types of erotic literature, *erotic realism* (ER) and *hard-core pornography* (HCP), Jakobovits suggested a number of criteria for distinguishing between the two:

1. Context: ER contains little or no story context surrounding the description of sexual activity, while HCP does develop a story line.

2. Exaggeration: ER strives for realism, while HCP contains so-called wish-fulfilling distortions.

3. Anti-erotic elements: These are present in ER absent in HCP.

When males and females were exposed to these two kinds of stories, females rated HCP as consistently more interesting and sexually exciting than ER; while males found ER more arousing than HCP.

Despite this conflict, the Jakobovits findings are consistent with those of Kinsey and Loiselle and Mollenauer, in that all studies suggest the significance of fantasy in feminine sexual arousal. Kinsey found that males reported the greatest response to direct representations of sexual activity, while females gave the highest rating to films and literature in which sexuality was embedded in a fantasy context. Perhaps the fantasy context of HCP, far-fetched though it generally is, constitutes the necessary arousal factor for females. Males, conversely, responding more readily to graphic and realistic erotica, find the direct descriptions of sexuality in ER most arousing.

Results of several recent experimental studies bear out these earlier conclusions regarding meaningful sex differences in response to erotic stimuli. Mosher (1970) conducted a study in which college men and women were shown two films developed at The Institute of Sex Research in Hamburg, Germany (Schmidt and Sigusch, 1970). These films portrayed the same man and woman in the same physical setting. In the film of coitus, the couple engaged in a sequence of undressing, kissing, manual genital petting, and face-to-face sexual intercourse. In the oral-genital sex film, the same preliminary sequence was shown followed by cunnilingus and fellatio to ejaculation.

After viewing the films, the subjects completed forms indicating their physiological and emotional reactions to the films, and rated the films as pornographic, disgusting, enjoyable, and so on. Mosher's data indicated that both sexes indicated equal arousal (in terms of reported physical sensations) to the coitus films, but males reported more arousal to the oral-genital films than females. On an emotional level, the females regarded behavior portrayed in the two films as more pornographic, disgusting, and offensive than did the male college students. But, as is not uncommon, their reactions were mixed — they experienced positive feelings of enjoyment along with their disgust. Generally, the male students reported more intensified feelings of arousal than did women. In brief, the immediate reactions to the film were moderate sexual arousal and sexual desire in men and heightened negative emotions in women. In a second poll taken twenty-four hours later, the two groups still differed in their reports of emotional reactions.

In a similar study carried out with thirty-two married couples, Mosher found that both males and females reported some enjoyment and stimulation, but the wives — like the female college students — were significantly less aroused by both films and rated the films as more disgusting and offensive than their husbands. Generally, Mosher's study supports the hypothesis that males and females will respond differently to portrayals of sexual activity, adding the significant corollary that women continue to find pornography distasteful even after marriage and the (probable) corresponding increase in sexual experience. The fact of these differences cannot be disputed; their origins are clearly a matter for further research.

It is conceivable, however, that these patterns are already undergoing significant alterations as a result of the Women's Liberation movement. As women of all classes become increasingly aware of their right to enjoy their own sexuality, these differences in the emotional reactions of men and women to erotica may soon be a thing of the past.

EDUCATIONAL-SOCIOECONOMIC LEVEL

We treat educational and economic levels as a single measure of social status, since there are few studies relating the educational variable to pornography. In the original Kinsey report (1948), it was noted that "the use of literature and erotic pictures for stimulation during masturbation is not really common, and it is largely confined to better-educated individuals" (p. 510). From their interviews with residents of penal institutions, Kinsey's researchers report that prisoners insist that little, if any, arousal results from conversations, printed pictures, descriptions in literature, or anything short of actual contact with a sexual partner. They attribute the varying arousal potentials of males with different educational backgrounds to two factors: accessibility of sexual partners for intercourse, and capacity of the individual to identify with symbolic situations.

Kinsey's data also indicate that upper-level (upper socioeconomic status) males report a minimum of premarital or extramarital intercourse. Deprived of actual sexual satisfaction, they report a higher incidence of premarital masturbation than lower-level males and a greater sensitivity to erotic stimuli. The lower-level male, however, has earlier access to sexual partners and reports less masturbation or sensitivity to erotic stimuli.

Kinsey and his associates suggest that the higher the male's educational level, the greater his capacity to fantasize. They found that for the most part, only fairly well-educated males were aroused by erotic literature and pictures. Lower-class males, by contrast, viewed the use of pictures or literature to augment masturbatory fantasies as the strangest sort of perversion. It is conceivable that, with the wider distribution of erotica in recent years, these social class differences in reactions to pornography are less clearly defined. In the underground days of the 1930s and 1940s, pornography was available only through illegal channels, and therefore expensive — only reasonably well-off males could afford it. Today, with less restrictive pornography laws and hence cheaper pornography, its appeal may well have transcended class lines.

Gebhard et al. (1965) make a similar point in their study of sexual offenders. Contrasting institutionalized sexual offenders with institutionalized nonsexual offenders, they found that the nonsexual offenders reported greater response to erotic stimuli. The nonsexual offenders were also better educated and younger than the sexual offenders. These researchers argue that strong response to pornography is associated with imaginativeness, ability to project, and sensitivity — all qualities that are encouraged by education. Since a deficiency in these same qualities is among the factors that distinguish sex offenders from nonsex offenders, the Gebhard report concludes that education accounts for the reported differences between these two groups in response to pornographic stimuli.

Unfortunately, the Kinsey and Gebhard reports rely heavily upon data from institutionalized individuals to support the importance of educational level. These individuals, by definition, are deprived of heterosexual contacts; thus, their reports of prior sexual feelings and activities may be colored by their need to inhibit sexual impulses while in prison. Certainly, it is reasonable to avoid erotic stimuli when no heterosexual outlets are available. Still, the importance of educational or social status in determining reactions to erotic stimuli is strongly suggested by these studies, and cannot be overlooked.

Sex Identity. Students of sexual behavior have emphasized the influence of early sex role models on the sexual behavior of adults. A male must identify with his biological peers if he is to develop appropriate patterns of heterosexual interest. Failure to identify can result in sexual confusion, homosexuality, or other problems of inadequate sexual orientation. Identification with the role of the opposite sex may be overt and conscious, as with the transsexual who feels himself to be of the opposite sex and desires that role, or covert and unconscious, in which case the individual inhibits or denies his "unnatural" impulses. Given the importance of this aspect of psychosexual development, it is necessary to explore its role in affecting reactions to erotic stimuli.

Miller and Swanson (1960) devised an experimental situation in which three groups of college men who tested at varying degrees of masculine identification were requested to examine photographs of attractive female nudes. Before and after the presentation of the photographs, each subject completed a set of stories for which the beginning had been supplied. Their responses were measured in accordance with the level of organization and clarity they attained in the two sets of stories. This test was designed to assess the subjects' ability to solve problems of interpersonal relationships. The results indicated that the less masculine subjects (men rated as "effeminate" and "unconsciously feminine") were prone to considerable disorganization in their fantasy problem-solving behavior following the presentation of the nude pictures. The men with high masculine identification performed as effectively after viewing the nude photographs as they had before seeing them. These findings suggest that males who are insecure in their masculine identification, or have rejected it entirely, are disturbed by exposure to a heterosexual erotic stimulus.

While not directly bearing on this issue, a study by Zamansky (1956) is worthy of note. He assessed sexual interest in terms of the amount of time that a subject spent examining each of two paired stimuli. While we cannot assume that homosexuals are invariably individuals with cross-sexed identification, they frequently manifest problems in sexual identity. Zamansky found that homosexual subjects spent a significantly longer time than heterosexual subjects in viewing pictures of men, in preference to pictures of women. More significantly, when pictures of females were paired with neutral pastoral scenes, the homosexuals continued to avoid looking at the female pictures. This active avoidance of female pictures, not representing nudes, suggests that males with identity problems may unconsciously dodge exposure to heterosexual stimuli in an effort to ward off the kind of behavioral disruption found by Miller and Swanson.

In a similar vein, Goldberg and Milstein (1965) studied the perceptual responses of female college students to sex pictures presented for increasingly long exposure times. The females had previously been tested and rated high or low on a scale of latent homosexuality (unconscious cross-sex identification). A series of stimuli (clothed male, clothed female, nude male, nude female, two nude females, and a neutral picture) were presented one at a time — first very briefly then for longer periods — until the subject correctly recognized each picture. Goldberg and Milstein found that the females rated as latent homosexuals took significantly longer to recognize the high threat (nude female, nude females) pictures than did the females with minimal homosexual tendencies. This study suggests that females, like males, will avoid threatening sexual stimuli when they are uncertain of their sexual identity.

Sex Guilt. A number of studies have related a person's level of sexual guilt to his reaction to erotic stimuli. "Sex guilt" refers to the person's guilt concerning his own sexual impulses and activities. In an early study on this problem, Leiman and Epstein (1961) studied the role of sexual guilt in determining fantasy responses to sexually relevant stimuli. Sixty unmarried men were tested as a group with a specially designed set of TAT-type cards and were subsequently asked to fill out a sex guilt questionnaire. The TAT-type pictures were designed to vary along a dimension of "sexual relevance"; for example, one picture depicted a man lying on a bed, embracing a woman and being kissed by her as she leaned over him (high sex relevance); another picture showed a young man sitting at a desk and writing a letter (low sex relevance).

The sex guilt inventory asked the man to rate as true or false such statements as: "I avoid sexy shows when I can." "It is wrong to indulge in sex strictly for pleasure." "I feel guilty about my sexual behavior." Lieman and Epstein found that subjects who reported low sexual guilt reacted to the high sex relevance cards with stories containing more direct sexual references than stories about the same cards by high guilt males. The stories about low sex relevance cards, as might be expected, did not vary from one group to the other. It is difficult to determine from the Leiman-Epstein data whether the high and low sex guilt subjects differ in their willingness to *perceive* sexual activities in the cards, or in their willingness to *report* the activities perceived. Other studies suggest that the latter interpretation is more accurate.

Mosher and Greenberg (1969) found that college women who tested high in sex guilt reported increases in the guilt level after reading an erotic literary passage, a significantly greater increase than that reported by low sex guilt women who read the same passage.

Mosher also attempted to connect scores on his sex guilt scale with responses to a sex attitudes and practices questionnaire originally published in *Psychology Today* magazine (Athanasiou and Shaver, 1969). He found, not surprisingly, that high sex guilt subjects had more conservative standards about premarital and extramarital sex, the dissemination of sexual information, contraceptive devices, and legalized abortions. They were more likely to frown on homosexuality and to believe that recent Supreme Court decisions about censorship and pornography threatened moral standards and that the government should strongly enforce existing sex laws. High sex guilt males were less likely to obtain pornography voluntarily and to report their responses to past exposure to pornography; and they were likely to experience guilt when reading sexy stories or looking at pictures of sex acts. The high sex guilt subjects were also more religiously and politically conservative than low sex guilt subjects.

The sex practices of high and low sex guilt subjects, according to their reports, differed in both quantity and quality. Generally, high sex guilt subjects reported that fear of social disapproval, guilt feelings, and religious or moral training kept them from freely expressing their sexuality.

In sum, these results suggest that high sex guilt prevents a person from seeking out erotic stimuli, real or symbolic. But what happens when he does encounter such stimuli inadvertently? Does he fail to become aroused, or does he become aroused and then feel guilty about it afterward?

In the 1970 study by Mosher discussed above, the reactions of subjects high and low in sex guilt to pornographic films were compared. Mosher did not relate sex guilt to the degree of reported sexual arousal after viewing the films. In evaluating the films, however, high sex guilt subjects rated the film as more pornographic, disgusting, and offensive than did low guilt subjects. While both males and females in the high sex guilt group were consistent in reporting these negative evaluations, the sexes differed in reports of other feelings. For example, all males, including those with high sex guilt, reported an increased feeling of happiness and eagerness for sexual contact with a woman after film viewing, while high sex guilt females did not. The high sex guilt subjects reported mild increases in internal unrest, nervousness, and guilt in the twenty-four hours after viewing a film in comparison to the day before. Thus, high sex guilt does not interfere with sexual arousal to erotic stimuli, but affects a person's reaction to this arousal in terms of acceptance or rejection. The high sex guilt individual generally avoids erotic stimuli, is aroused by them when he encounters them, and feels disgusted and devalued afterward. He appears to project his reactions onto others, feeling that they should be prevented from seeing erotic stimuli, as they will share his reaction sequence of arousal followed by disgust and shame. Certain sex differences are confirmed by Mosher's data, in that high sex guilt males report a desire for sexual contact after film viewing though they feel guilty about this desire. The high guilt females differ from low guilt females in failing to report this sexual desire.

Other data reported by Mosher suggest that the above findings apply to single, largely sexually inexperienced individuals, but not to married and sexually experienced individuals. In showing the same films to thirty-two married couples, Mosher found a different correlation between sex guilt and film reactions. The sharp differences between single males and females in ratings of disgust did not appear between male and female married subjects.

Mosher found that married females who tested high in sex guilt reported increased guilt feelings after seeing the films, as did the high guilt single college females in the 1969 Mosher-Greenberg study after reading an erotic passage.

The high sex guilt married male, however, differed markedly from his single counterpart, reporting more stimulation and less guilt than the low sex guilt married males. Other data on the sex practices of these high sex guilt married males bears on their positive reactions to pornography. Generally, they and their wives reported less satisfaction in sexual relations than low sex guilt couples, and the males had masturbated more frequently than low guilt married males over the previous six months. Mosher hypothesizes that masturbation and pornography provide an outlet for the high sex guilt married male who is unable to enjoy sex with his wife — perhaps because he envisions her as a "good, pure woman" who cannot provide the stimulation he finds in pornographic fantasies.

Prior Sexual Experience. There is little data on the question of whether a person's prior experience with a type of sex act affects his reaction to a symbolic representation of that act. In a sense the studies analyzed above suggest that it probably does: high sex guilt males report less varied sexual activity after marriage, and greater positive response to films of sexual activities not experienced in their marriage. This suggests a compensatory mechanism in which the taboo element combines with inexperience to function as an exciting erotic stimulus. A study by Levitt and Hinesley (1967), however, fails to confirm this hypothesis. They found that when male graduate students rated photos of various erotic activities for their arousal value, there was no direct correlation between lack of experience and intensity of arousal. But, as noted above, photos of erotic activity constitute a very limited stimulus, and the influence of prior sexual experience should be tested by means of more elaborate stimuli, in which complex themes are represented.

LONG-TERM EFFECTS OF PORNOGRAPHY

All the studies reviewed thus far deal primarily with immediate, short-run reactions to erotic stimuli. Current social concern, however, focuses on more long-range effects, such as shifts in sex attitudes, practices, and values, and few studies to date have been directed at this issue. Mosher's 1970 study, in which college students viewed erotic films, is relevant here, but only to a degree. Mosher found that with single college students, women reported more instances of internal unrest, gastrointestinal complaints, and nervousness than the men, when tested twenty-four hours after seeing the films. There was little effect on the sexual behavior of these students, aside from a reported increase in conversations and fantasies about sex during that twenty-four-hour period. The married couples reported a significant increase in petting and intercourse in the twenty-four hours following the film; however, there were no increases in novel sexual behavior or extramarital behavior.

Thus, it appears that the sexual arousal qualities of an erotic film reinforce a person's current sexual pattern. Where continuous sexuality is not part of the pattern, no increase in direct sexual activity is noted (as in the single students), but sexuality is expressed indirectly, through fantasies and conversations. For the married couples, regular sexual activity is part of the sanctioned lifestyle, and the film does stimulate greater sexual activity. The activity, however, is not modeled after that shown in the film, but simply repeats previously established patterns of sexual behavior. An erotic film appears to stimulate a state of nonspecific sexual arousal, which is filtered through a person's normal controls and inhibitions before any behavioral expression occurs. Whether this controlled reaction is experienced by disturbed individuals, as by the relatively well-adjusted individuals in Mosher's study, remains to be demonstrated.

Mosher, attempting to measure changes in sex attitudes two weeks after exposure to the film, found that, for more sexually experienced single subjects, opinions about premarital sex became slightly more liberal. Perhaps reflecting certain vested interests, the single subjects failed to modify their high conservative attitudes concerning extramarital sex, while the married subjects, predictably more liberal about extramarital sex, did not alter their opinions about premarital sex. These findings indicate that an individual interprets erotic stimuli in terms of their relevance to his current life situation.

Other studies which have attempted to touch on this problem of long-term effects of pornography have been retrospective in nature. That is, researchers have examined certain deviant groups in order to determine whether their contact with pornography differentiated them from more normal control groups. Gebhard et al. (1965) studies the sexual histories of a large sample of institutionalized sex offenders. A few of their questions, directed to 1,500 institutionalized sex offenders, 888 institutionalized nonsex offenders, and 477 noninstitutionalized controls, concerned exposure to pornography. The subjects were asked to report the degree of sexual arousal that resulted from viewing pictures of sexual activities. Twenty-eight percent of the sex criminals reported strong arousal, but so did 34 percent of the noninstitutionalized controls. Thirty-six percent of the controls stated that they were aroused only slightly or not at all, but 43 percent of the sex offenders were similarly unaffected.

Certain differences did appear between types of sex offenders and control groups. The child molesters and the controls reported the highest arousal from erotic stimuli, while the rapists and homosexuals reported the least arousal to heterosexual pictures. Since these groups also differed in age, degree of sexual deprivation, and education, the differences between groups often reduced to these more basic variables.

Gebhard et al. conclude from their study, "It would appear that the possession of pornography does not differentiate sex offenders from nonsex offenders. Even the combination of ownership plus strong sexual arousal from the material does not segregate the sex offender from others of comparable social level."

A problem that arises in studying reactions to pornography among sex offenders is that they appear to generate their own pornography from nonsexual stimuli. For example, Lindner (1953) compared the reactions of a group of sex offenders with those of a group of nonsex offenders to sexually stimulating, nonsexually stimulating, and neutral pictures. Subjects took the Serial Drawing Test and the Incomplete Pictures Test, both involving pictures that were ambiguous with regard to sexual connotations. The sex offenders deduced a significantly greater number of sexual activities from the drawings (children playing near a tree, figure petting a dog, and three people standing unrelated to each other) than did the nonsex offenders. They also were more prone to incorporate recently viewed sexual pictures into a series of gradually more explicit drawings. These results imply that the sex offender is highly receptive to sexual stimuli, and reads sexual meanings into images that would be devoid of erotic connotations for the normal person. Certainly, this finding was borne out by our study of institutionalized pedophiles (child molesters), who found the familiar suntan lotion ad showing a young child, with buttocks exposed to reveal his sunburn as a dog pulls at his bathing suit, to be one of most erotic stimuli they had encountered.

This ability of the sex deviate to "create" his own pornography is further documented by Goldhirsh (1961) who found that the dreams of sex offenders more frequently contained sexual elements than the dreams of nonsex offenders. In fact, seven of the eight sex offenders had one or more dreams containing an uncamouflaged sex crime theme, which was totally absent from the control group's dreams.

The few existing studies on long-term effects of exposure to pornography have focused on the response of sex offenders to erotic stimuli as adults. No really good studies exist that attempt to trace and relate early experiences with pornography to later sexual adjustment. We decided, therefore, that this was to be the major focus of our research project. Such an investigation requires a longitudinal approach, best accomplished through an intensive interview technique along the lines established by Kinsey. Therefore, the first phase of our project involved the development of a clinical research instrument designed to probe, in depth, each subject's exposure to pornography at different points in his life; and to trace some of the behavioral and attitudinal consequences of this exposure.

SUMMARY AND CONCLUSIONS

While the literature reviewed above does not always deal with the kind of erotic stimuli that we currently term *pornographic,* certain trends are clearly identifiable:

1. There appear to be marked sex differences in the type of erotic stimuli found exciting.

2. Females and males seem to experience equal sexual arousal to most stimuli, but females also experience concurrent negative emotions that males (except those high in sex guilt) do not experience.

3. The context of exposure to erotica plays a significant role in its sexual arousal value. This is true for the social context (others present, place of exposure, etc.) as well as contextual cues within the erotic material (the perceived intentions of the creator, the taboo nature of the book or pictures, etc.).

4. Sex guilt plays a significant factor in determining emotional and behavioral reactions to erotic stimuli. The greater the sex guilt, the greater the conflict that will be experienced and the less likely it becomes that behavior described in the erotica will be imitated.

5. Sexual identification influences response to erotica, in terms of type of stimuli found arousing and impact of the stimuli. Generally, those men who identify closely with their own sex report stronger arousal from heterosexual erotica than those with weaker identification. The reverse seems true for females: the strongest response to erotica was found in females with pronounced cross-sex identification.

6. Sex offenders and nonheterosexuals do not appear to report greater use of erotica than various comparison groups. Variations in usage within these samples are closely related to educational level.

7. Studies on the impact of exposure to erotica on subsequent sexual

behavior have generally covered only a brief period after the exposure. The principal conclusion of these experimental studies has been that subsequent sexual behavior is a function of the availability of a sanctioned sexual partner. The results are very different for single as compared to married subjects. The effects for married individuals are short-lived and minimal and rarely indicate variations from the regular patterns of sexual behavior.

3

DEVELOPMENT OF THE CLINICAL RESEARCH INSTRUMENT

The first step in our investigation of the impact of erotic stimuli on sexual behavior involved the construction of a comprehensive interview that could elicit facts, attitudes, fantasies, and behavior surrounding exposure to erotica at different periods in a person's life. We attempted to develop an in-depth interview, that is, a series of questions designed to probe intensively into emotional reactions and subsequent behavior, and repetitive enough to permit estimates of a respondent's veracity. Clearly, our approach to the construction of the interview was influenced by two major sources: (1) the reports of the Kinsey researchers on their experiences in obtaining valid sexual histories, and (2) our accumulated experience in interviewing patients, using a psychoanalytic model involving indispensable techniques for stimulating recall.

Based on our review of the literature, certain variables seemed to be significant in the study of the effects of pornography. Using these leads, we developed a schematic model outlining the various factors that might affect an individual's reactions to pornography. This model is illustrated in table 4.

We then attempted to develop an interview schedule that would permit us to evaluate these factors in a systematic fashion. As indicated in

Table 4

MODEL OF FACTORS AFFECTING REACTIONS TO PORNOGRAPHY

Factors Occurring Prior to Exposure That Condition Reactions	Stimulus	Context of Exposure	Immediate Reactions	Longer Term Reactions
Antecedent Factors: Demographic 1) Age 2) Educational-social status level 3) Sex 4) Religious background 5) Marital status *Antecedent Factors: Personal* 1) Prior sexual experience 2) Prior experience with erotica 3) Sex attitudes 4) Sex identification conflict 5) Sex guilt 6) Quality of current sex life	1) Media (photo, book, film) 2) Content (nudity, heterosexual intercourse, homosexual activity, etc.) 3) Themes presented ("The seduction of the innocent," etc.) 4) Artistic level of stimulus (erotic realism, hard-core pornography)	1) Alone or with others 2) Relationship of others present to viewer (peer, someone in authority) 3) Social setting of exposure (party, school, home) 4) Both sexes or only one in group 5) Number of erotic stimuli (if any) viewed just before exposure	1) Sexual arousal 2) Disgust 3) Shame 4) Boredom (following repetitive exposure to erotica) 5) Increase in sex fantasies	1) Shifts in sex attitudes 2) Shifts in quantity and/or quality of sex practices 3) Aggression 4) Shifts in attitudes toward erotica 5) Shifts in attitudes toward punishment of sex crimes

table 4, we perceive response to pornography as a function of various influences prior to exposure: demographic and personal; the nature of the erotic stimulus; and the context of exposure. Immediate reactions may be confined to specific feelings or desires, while long-term effects may involve changes in attitudes, behavior, or values. Our interview was designed to tie in with each of these factors often, in the sequence depicted in table 4.

Our basic task in this research was to examine the quantity and quality of each subject's experience with erotic material, utilizing the interview format. We felt that a substantial interview which probed the respondent's reactions in detail would reveal more valuable data than a precoded format. We recognized the problems inherent in coding open-ended responses, but felt that in an initial exploratory study breadth of response was more significant than precision of scoring. We therefore decided to code the interview on an empirical basis after a sufficient number of interviews (at least 50) had been obtained.

It is possible to survey many aspects of a respondent's experience with pornography. We decided, given the importance of developmental issues described above, to sample three time periods: the preadolescent years (six to twelve), the adolescent period (thirteen to eighteen), and the year immediately prior to the interview, representing a sample of adult experience. We recognized that the earlier the recollection, the more likely that details will be forgotten, repressed, or distorted by the interviewee. The work of Kinsey and his associates suggested, however, that carefully defined questions presented in different versions during an interview could elicit stable reports of early sexual experiences. Also, we were greatly influenced by the advice of one of our consultants on the project, William Simon, who argued that adolescent experiences with erotica are vivid moments, readily recalled by a respondent.

Validation of Responses. The model presented in table 4 helped determine the nature and order of questions in the clinical research instrument. The exact pattern of the interview was based on additional considerations, such as the need to devise a format that began by soliciting innocuous information and gradually tapped more personal reactions. We also attempted to have the respondent report on the *frequency* of his experiences with erotica, before investigating his *reactions* and *behavior* subsequent to the experience. Thus, a subject would go on record as having seen a particular type of stimulus *before* being asked about his reactions to it. Pilot research had indicated that if we inquired about these matters concurrently, subject defensiveness would increase markedly throughout the interview.

The separation of reports of exposure to erotica from reports of emotional and behavioral reactions permitted us to verify, to some extent, the data reported in each section. Thus, a subject would be asked, "Have you ever seen a film depicting sexual intercourse?" and, if his answer was affirmative, "How many?" He might answer, "Never." Later, during the probe of "peak" experiences with pornography, he would be asked which experience stood out most in his mind, and he might answer, "A film showing intercourse." At this point, the interviewer could explore the discrepancy between these two replies to determine which was more accurate. Throughout the interview, similar questions were asked in a number of different forms to check a respondent's reliability of report.

Developmental Progression of Interview Sections. Another aspect of the design of the interview involves the progression from preadolescent to recent experience. The interview begins with an attempt to put the subject at ease and to introduce him to questions dealing with his experiences with pornography. Following this is a brief section concerned with exposure and reactions to exposure during the preadolescent years.

To illustrate the flow of questions and the types of answers elicited, a sample of two interviews focused on preadolescent exposure to erotica follows.

INT.	RESP. 1	RESP. 2
Often when kids are growing up, that is, in their preadolescent period (between 6 and 12 years old), they come across materials in which nude people are shown or described. What did you come across?	Well, it was when I was about nine or ten, my brother and myself came across some pictures of a woman doing a strip-tease. It was a photograph.	I think three or four books [my dad — used to take in nude movie pictures] and when I knew what was happening, I knew what they were.
Who showed it to you?	Nobody really, my father had left them laying around the house and we discovered them.	I think I just found it at home.
Who were you with?	My brother.	I was always alone when I looked at it and felt very guilty about it.

INT.	RESP. 1	RESP. 2
What did you learn from it?	I don't know really, I guess what I might have learned from it was what a nude woman looked like.	I don't think I learned anything. I think I got pretty fantastic ideas of what sex should be like — that sort of thing you know — it's all pretty glorified.
Did you learn anything about sex from this (picture or movie)?	No, I can't say that I did.	That's where I got my sex education. The thing that keeps running through my mind when I think about it, it's the inflated opinion I got of what the sex act ends up as.
Was there anything you found out about sex from this experience that you later learned was not so?	No, I don't think so.	I later learned that you don't see stars or hear bells when you have sex, like it seemed then.
Did you do anything of a sexual nature after seeing that (picture or movie)?	Not that I can remember.	I masturbated a lot. [Int.: Even at this age?] I matured really early and I can remember being sexually aroused in the fourth grade.

This section of the interview then goes on to explore whether the respondent saw anything of an explicitly sexual nature during his pre-adolescent years and what emotions and actions, if any, followed this exposure.

After this section, the interviewer would shift to adolescence, with questions concerning the respondent's frequency of exposure to various types of pornographic stimuli. The respondent was asked to indicate how many of these stimuli he encountered as a teenager, and generally how he came across them. He was questioned in detail about various pornographic media such as photos, books, and films, and about his exposure to a range of sexual stimuli in each medium, varying from partial nudity through sadomasochistic practices. Based on the research of Levitt and Hinesley (1967) depicted in table 2, we felt we could not define any one type of stimulus as more erotic or pornographic than another. It seemed more important to visualize the degree of explicitness of erotic stimuli as a continuum with partial nudity at one end, as the least explicit stimulus, and sadomasochism at the other, as the most explicit. After the interviewer mentioned a stimulus, the respondent was asked to estimate how many examples of that stimulus, if any, he had encountered during his adolescent years. These frequency estimates played an important role in later comparisons of different target groups.

Once again a sample of the questions and replies may help the reader appreciate the mode of questioning:

INT.: *Now, thinking about your adolescence, do you remember having seen photographs, drawings, or cartoons of nude women?*
RESP.: Yes, there were a number of those little comic books passed around in school.

INT.: *How many did you see during your teenage years?*
RESP.: About ten all told.

INT.: *What about photographs of nude women showing their sex organs?*
RESP.: Yes, I remember some black-and-white photos that I saw one summer at camp.

INT.: *How many photos of this type did you see during your teenage years?*
RESP.: About fifteen.

INT.: *How about photos of nude males?*
RESP.: I can't remember seeing any at all.

This section of the interview would proceed through all types of stimuli representing all types of sexual activity.

The frequency estimates were important in and of themselves, but they were also designed to prod the subject's memory for experiences with erotica during his teenage years. At some point, he was asked to recall his most vivid or "peak" experience, the one that stood out most in his mind as a teenager. Ordinarily, there was an immediate response to this question, indicating ready availability of a vivid experience. Our concern with the "peak" experience reflected our conviction that these experiences were most likely to relate to sharp shifts in attitudes, values, and sexual behavior.

Intensive questioning followed the isolation of a peak experience, according to the original model (table 4). At this stage, the situational factors, dispositional factors, nature of the stimulus, subject's reactions, and long-term consequences were examined in great detail. A sample of questions and answers on these matters follows:

INT.: *Of all these photographs, films, and books that you have mentioned seeing during your teens, which really stands out?*

RESP.: A photo of a girl with her dress up showing thighs, vulva — no panties.

INT.: *What about the photo makes it stand out in your mind so strongly?*

RESP.: The girl was pretty, smiling, she enjoyed what she was doing — she was pretty, cute. The girl was fully dressed and this made the picture more erotic. It made me feel that I was sneaking a look at her.

INT.: *Where did you see the photo?*

RESP.: Along a roadside.

INT.: *What about the photo of the girl was sexually exciting?*

RESP.: The girl's personal warmth — also the poor focus and fuzziness of the photo made it more exciting.

INT.: *People often have more than one reaction, both pleasant and unpleasant, to a photo like that; what were your other feelings?*

RESP.: No others.

INT.: *Did anything about the photo disgust you?*

RESP.: No, I felt almost in love with the photo, in fact.

After a series of questions concerning his age at the time of exposure and whether anyone saw the picture with him, the respondent was asked:

INT.: *Was there anything about sex in the photo that you had never heard of before?*

RESP.: It was the first time that I ever had a close look at a woman's sex organs.

INT.: *What about sex did you learn from the photo?*

RESP.: Nothing.

After a series of other questions, the respondent was asked:

INT.: *Was there anything shown or described in the photo that you wished to try later?*

RESP.: Yes, straight [sic] intercourse.

INT.: *Did you try it?*

RESP.: No, I didn't have anyone to try it with.

Later in this section of the interview, the questions dealt with the incorporation of images, attitudes, and so forth, derived from the erotica into the person's teen-age sex fantasies.

INT.: *In what ways did scenes from these movies, books, or photographs come to be part of your daydreams or thoughts? Would any specific scenes come to mind while daydreaming?*

RESP.: I often pictured myself with girls in the photos, sometimes as their husband.

INT.: *We know from Kinsey and similar studies that almost all kids masturbate during their teens. How often did thinking or dreaming about any of these materials excite you to masturbate?*

RESP.: About once a week.

INT.: *Did you usually masturbate while looking at the material or just thinking about it?*

RESP.: I usually would think about the picture, then elaborate a little story in my mind based on a scene in the picture while masturbating.

Following this section, the interview focused upon the subject's experiences with erotica during the year prior to the interview. The estimates of frequency of exposure to sexual stimuli in each medium of presentation (photos, books, etc.) were garnered again for this time period. Following this, the respondent was asked once again to describe his "peak" experience with pornography during the previous year; he is then questioned about it in considerable detail, more so than for his adolescent experience.

Continuing with the same respondent as above, the interviewer attempted to select and probe the impact of a recent peak experience.

INT.: *Of all these photographs, movies, books, and live shows that you have seen in the past year, which really stands out in your mind most?*

RESP.: A movie seen at a friend's house.

INT.: *What about the movie makes it stand out in your mind so strongly?*

RESP.: It was a 35 mm movie of good quality about a young couple in love having intercourse, both oral and genital. The sensitivity of approach, the portrayal of a believable, sincere approach to sex really made it stand out for me.

INT.: *Where did you see it?*

RESP.: In a private sound stage.

INT.: *Were you using alcohol, pot, or other stuff at the time?*

RESP.: No.

INT.: *What about sex did you learn from this?*

RESP.: Nothing — just a good attitude toward sex.

INT.: *Was there anything shown or described in the movie that you wished you could try later?*

RESP.: Not in this movie. I did learn some new positions that I wanted to try in other movies.

The next section of the interview involved the most intimate questions of all. In an effort to relate experience with erotic material to the development and reinforcement of recurring sex fantasies, we developed a section on sex fantasy. In this section, the respondent was asked in detail about his recurring sex fantasies and then questioned concerning their possible origins in his experiences with pornographic materials. Also, he was questioned concerning the use of erotic material to sustain or realize the fantasies in his actual sexual activity. Attempts to use fantasies, stimulated by erotica, to shape relations with sexual partners were probed with particular care. Again, a sample of an interview may clarify our method.

INT.: *Most people find it more exciting to have daydreams or fantasies about sex. You know, thinking about sexual experiences that have happened or making up experiences that have not happened. Some people find it exciting to daydream about these things before having sex and others like to continue imagining throughout the sex act. Are your sex fantasies or daydreams always pretty much the same or do they vary?*

RESP.: They are always pretty much the same, but they vary in detail, you know, the content, who I'm thinking about — that sort of thing.

INT.: *What is happening in your fantasy?*

RESP.: The basic plot would be where somehow or other I would seduce some girl I know — and would go through some mad, passionate makeout scene with pretty free caressing and kissing everywhere and oral copulation and all that. And then we would have sex and it would be tremendous and she would love me forever because I was such a good lover. And I would love her forever because she was so good.

INT.: *Do you have sex fantasies during the sex act?*

RESP.: No, I'm generally too involved.

INT.: *In your sex fantasies do you think about someone you know or some other person?*

RESP.: Generally, someone I know, maybe not someone I know intimately but someone I know, a real person.

INT.: *Do you find daydreams more exciting during the sex act, or before?*

RESP.: Maybe, before and after. I sort of lived from one to the next. I didn't do any daydreaming when I was actually involved with a woman.

INT.: *As part of your current sexual life, in what ways do you use books, pictures, films, and other materials to arouse yourself?*

RESP.: I used to read books and masturbate.

Following this section of the interview, the interviewer lists a series of discrete sex fantasies of various types and asks the respondent whether these have been part of his daydreaming pattern.

INTERVIEWER   RESPONDENT

Do you ever have fantasies about:

  (a) *heterosexual intercourse with your partner?*   Yes

  (b) *oral-genital activity?*   No

  (c) *homosexual acts?*   Yes

  (d) *whipping and spanking or forcing people to do something they don't want to do?*   No

  (e) *being whipped or spanked or forced to do something you don't want to do?*   No

  (f) *being dressed in clothes of the opposite sex?*   No

  (g) *how about sex with a person other than the one you are making love to?*   Yes

  (h) *sex involving many different people?*   Yes

  (i) *with animals?*   No

INT.: *To what extent have you been able to find books, pictures or films which vividly portrayed your favorite sex daydreams?*

RESP.: I think, all of them, really — it was easy.

In the final section of the interview, the respondent was questioned about his general sex attitudes, his perceptions of his parents' attitudes on sex, and current sex practices. It was felt, as table 4 suggests, that these are important variables influencing reactions to pornography. These questions were placed at the end of the interview to ensure that the general positions expressed would not influence the subject's descriptions of his responses to erotic material. It seemed less likely that descriptions of experiences with pornographic stimuli would alter expressions of general sex attitudes. We are indebted to Dr. William Simon for providing us with the sex attitude and practices items derived from his large-scale surveys of sexual behavior.

Table 5 provides an overall picture of the interview, naming the divisions of each section and indicating the number of questions in each division. The entire interview is reproduced in appendix A.

Reduction of Data into Quantitative Form. As the above samples suggest, an interview of this length and intensity harvests a great deal of rich and informative data from every person questioned. To compress this data so that it could be analyzed quantitatively and qualitatively, we developed an elaborate system of objective coding categories that could be applied by minimally trained coders with high reliability. In the chapters that follow, we shall present statistical analyses of the data which permit us to compare the various groups in our study, interspersed with segments of actual interviews to provide a profile of the people who shared their intimate thoughts and feelings with us.

Table 5

THE STRUCTURE OF THE INTERVIEW

	Section 1			
	Introductory Statement	*Demographic Data*	*Warm-up Questions*	*Preadolescent Experience*
Questions	—	1–19	20–25	26–48

	Section 2			
	Specific Frequencies of Exposure (Adolescence)	*Analysis of Peak Experience (Adolescence)*	*Specific Frequencies of Exposure (Recent)*	*Analysis of Peak Experience (Recent)*
Questions	49–75	76–127	128–163	164–215

	Section 3			
	Role of Fantasy	*Sex Attitudes*	*Sex History and Practices*	*General Attitudes Toward Pornography*
Questions	217–239	241–257	258–272	273–276

Let me tell you about
The 120 Days of Sodom
by the Marquis de Sade.
I was a senior in college and a friend of mine had a copy of it
in his apartment and I started glancing through it. I was thoroughly disgusted
with it and I put it down and refused to open the book again.
It was a nauseating and sick book written,
I would have to say, by a very very sick person who
removes sex totally out of the area of pleasant intimacy
between two human beings to that of complete disgust.
However, I would not go so far as to say
that this book should be taken off the shelves and
burned or banned. I will leave it there
and not bother with it. If somebody else
wants to come along and read it, and
get turned on by it, more power to him.
He probably needs a little help.

A CONTROL SUBJECT

4

SELECTION OF THE
SAMPLES TO BE INTERVIEWED

Most people, if they were honest, would agree that age-old assumptions about man's sexual corruptibility retain their appeal from century to century. The authors of the Bible cautioned youths to shun wine and whores, noting that one was likely to lead to the other. Puritan garb attempted to desexualize the body, just as fear of the torments of hell was supposed to restrain wayward thoughts. According to a 1917 book on sex, one-half of the youth in our prisons and houses of correction started on their evil careers by reading bad books. "These books are the nicotine and alcohol of literature; they poison and burn . . . the head and the heart as surely as their cousins do the stomach." *

But it was just this tenacious assumption, heretofore unassailable, which we wished to examine, armed with our completed interview outline. The least ambiguous, most direct method for estimating the long-term effects of erotica upon sexual attitudes and behavior would be to

* Quoted in *Psychology Today* (December 1970): 59.

utilize a longitudinal study, with systematic control over the conditions of exposure to erotica. Since such studies are difficult to carry out and involve many years of investigation before the data are available, we compromised by deciding on the retrospective study. We felt that investigating the backgrounds of individuals known to be sex offenders, nonheterosexuals, or heavy users of pornography might provide clues as to whether early exposure to erotica was related to the development of such practices. While the results of retrospective interview studies are not unimpeachable, Kinsey's work has shown that they can yield valuable data.

Our primary concern was how exposure to erotica might relate to a pattern of antisocial sexuality. Therefore, we decided to investigate the histories of exposure to erotica of individuals convicted for sexual offenses. Recognizing from other research that the process of arrest and incarceration has major effects on the individual's attitudes and feelings, we also wished to locate unincarcerated people whose sexual practices might have led to imprisonment had they been observed by law enforcement authorities. Accordingly, we selected a sample of noninstitutionalized homosexuals and a sample of transsexuals for inclusion in the study. Since the focus of our investigation was on pornography, we also wished to examine the consequences of using these materials for people acknowledged to be heavy consumers of erotica, and a sample of this group was included as well.

The data from all of these sample groups require some control or baseline data for contrast. We attempted to define such a group and to match it to the characteristics of the institutionalized sex offenders in particular. The groups selected and their prominent demographic characteristics are described below.

SAMPLE 1: INSTITUTIONALIZED SEX OFFENDERS*

A sex offender is a person who has been legally convicted as a result of an overt act, committed by him for his own sexual gratification, that is contrary to the laws of the community in which he lives. Our sample of male sex offenders was obtained with the generous cooperation of the research and psychology staffs at Atascadero State Hospital, a California institution for the "criminally insane."

The inmates of Atascadero are there because they do not qualify for

---

* Although one segment of the sex offender group — the male object pedophiles — qualifies as nonheterosexual, for our purposes throughout this book the term "nonheterosexuals" will refer only to (a) homosexuals preferring adult partners and (b) transsexuals.

the more lenient terms of probation, or the stricter and more dismal prospect of criminal custody. After a ninety-day period involving physical and psychiatric tests and daily observance, the clinical staff sifts out the nonmedically disordered as well as those medically disordered but not amenable to treatment. Those who remain are considered a potentially rehabilitatable group drawn from the total population of males arrested for sex crimes in California. These men, generally whites between the age of twenty and forty, come from every state in the nation. Forty-five percent are married but a large portion (69%) never graduated from high school, nor have they managed to hold a fairly steady job (for six months or more) in semiskilled or skilled manual employment. While their crimes included child molesting, rape or assault, incest, sodomy, and sex perversion, 69 percent were heterosexual offenses, often involving multiple victims. Single males (42%) were more prone to homosexual offenses with children than married males (12%). About 74 percent pleaded guilty in court to the crime of which they had been accused.

We wanted subjects who had not been long institutionalized and whose offenses included a range of aggressive sexual crimes. The hospital staff met our requirements by choosing a sample that contained, ultimately, twenty aggressive sexual offenders (hereafter referred to as *rapists*), twenty pedophiles preferring male objects, and twenty pedophiles whose victims were females. After being selected, each patient was informed about the aims of the project, reassured that all data would be confidential, and paid five dollars for participation.

After drawing the Atascadero sample, we compared it demographically to two other sex offender groups described in research literature. Both Gebhard et al. (1956) and Frisbie (1969) had used samples in excess of 1,000 subjects exclusive of controls. Pitting our small sample against theirs was a gamble that paid off handsomely.

The Gebhard study formulated nine categories of sex offenses based on three factors: (1) the sex of the victim (same or opposite), (2) the force used (consent or aggression), and (3) the age (adult, child twelve or under, minor twelve to sixteen. In order to make our comparison, we treated Gebhard's aggressive heterosexual offender, adult, as a rapist; his homosexual offender, child and minor, as male object pedophile; and his heterosexual offender, child or minor, as female object pedophile. The demographic match, based on these modified tables, was close, especially between rapists. Our percentage of female object pedophiles was double that in Gebhard's sample. In terms of marital status, we had twice as many married rapists and half as many single. The same trend applied to each of the other samples except that both groups had similar percentages (55–57%) of single male object pedophile.

As before, education proved to be the one unmatched variable. While in our sample, all the rapists had some high school, almost 45 percent of Gebhard's did not. About 10 percent of our sample did not enter high school, as against over 50 percent in the Gebhard study. Two factors could account for this; first, the general lack of educational opportunity fifteen years ago; second, the nature of the California education system which allows just about anyone to attend junior college. Whatever the reason, the education imbalance is reflected in socioeconomic data. Our more educated sample contained 10.5 percent unskilled workers as opposed to Gebhard's 47 percent, and 36.8 percent skilled to his 16 percent. With respect to sex, age, education, race, religion, marital status, and patterns of sexuality, our match with Frisbie to data based upon institutionalized sex offenders in California is reassuringly similar.

SAMPLE 2: HOMOSEXUALS

Since, for purposes of our study, we asked only that an individual define himself as a homosexual, we were able to approach volunteers through their membership in a local homophile organization, such as One, Incorporated. Our staff attended its annual dinner in order to describe the project and solicit subjects. We eventually obtained thirty-seven who were each paid ten dollars for their help. It was not possible to match the homosexual and sex offender samples in terms of education level, as the groups varied markedly from each other, with the homosexuals possessing generally higher educational levels. Nor can we know how representative our sample is of the general homosexual population, since it includes only those emancipated individuals who join clubs and accept public recognition of their status.

SAMPLE 3: TRANSSEXUALS

Transsexualism, the desire to change one's sex by actual surgical conversion, is gradually becoming a valid subject for medical research. Dr. Harry Benjamin, a psychiatrist who has done a great deal of work with transsexuals, calls the phenomenon a problem of gender identity and gender role orientation. Because the individual feels himself (or herself) to be a biological prisoner, the sex organs become objects of disgust and the individual makes persistent requests for removal and alteration through operation.

The subjects for our study came from the Gender Indentity Clinic of the University of California at Los Angeles. Each person applying for a sex-change treatment at UCLA is referred to the Gender Identity Clinic for psychiatric and psychological evaluation. We asked those clinic patients currently residing in the Los Angeles area to participate in our study. No patient who was contacted refused to participate. Each respondent was paid ten dollars for participation. The sample consists of thirteen males.

SAMPLE 4: PORNOGRAPHY USERS

It was our intention to obtain a sampling of persons in three categories: customers who frequent "adult" bookstores, patrons of "skinflick" movie theaters (i.e., theaters showing erotic movies exclusively), and persons whose names are on mailing lists of those who sell eight-millimeter erotic movies. While these groups proved difficult to approach, we did obtain a fair sample of subjects who craved pornographic stimulation and were persistent in searching it out.

By placing flyers describing our research in various adult bookstores and skinflick theaters in the Santa Monica and Hollywood areas of Los Angeles, we attracted customers hooked on both mediums to participate in our study. An advertisement in the Los Angeles *Free Press,* a local "underground" newspaper with large circulation, brought us a generous response from users who obviously hankered for the "enlightened censorship legislation" we cited as one of our goals. Unfortunately, our attempts to insert the ad in conventional newspapers and thus tap a different reading audience were unsuccessful, largely because editors considered our ad too controversial.

Through a wife-swapping association calling itself 101 we drew a few subjects who tended to be heavy users of pornography. They were also well educated and fairly affluent. We were unable, however, to discover any habitual users of eight-millimeter films willing to expose themselves even to the sworn anonymity of our coded interview. Thus, our final sample of seventy-eight, while less varied than we had hoped, still included important factions of the porno-seeking public.

THE BLACK SAMPLES

To allow for the possibility that a certain percentage of the sex offender sample would be black, we prepared black samples in the community at large for control purposes. The President's Commission on Pornography and Obscenity had stressed its preference, wherever possible, for studies encompassing all available cultural and racial identities in our population. Through contact with the Community Skills Center, Gardena, California, we were able to draw in twenty-two low-income males then participating in a training program for hard-core unemployed. Some of our staff members acquainted with the black community selected for us seventeen males whose income qualified them as "middle class" — and who also matched the age distribution of the Atascadero sample. As the sex offender group ultimately emerged as 95 percent white, we decided to utilize the black control data for contrast with the white control data. Except for some differences between black and white control groups in degree of preadolescent exposure to erotica, no marked differences appeared. Therefore, data for the black control group is presented in subsequent chapters only where it differs significantly from that of the white controls.

THE CONTROLS

In any study of this kind, it is essential to include some baseline data against which to compare findings with the special samples. The problem of defining and selecting a control sample is a formidable one. To ensure that the sample would be selected in an unbiased manner, we awarded a subcontract to the UCLA Survey Research Center. Given the age distribution and educational level of the Atascadero samples, they were told to locate a community sample matched on these parameters. There were two reasons to seek a match for the Atascadero samples. One was the priority rating assigned to a sound and reliable analysis of the sex criminal data. Accurate sampling from the general public would solidify our conclusions. And the other reason was that at the time we selected the controls, the Atascadero sample was the only one of the four subject groups we had completed. Using the Atascadero demographic data, the Research Center picked certain target areas of Los Angeles as likely to yield white males of the proper age range and educational level. Like the prison sample, the control group was to be almost exclusively white and Christian.

The UCLA Survey Research Center then selected specific streets on a random basis within these target areas, and conducted a house-to-house survey to locate respondents fitting our criteria and willing to participate. Of the 133 prospective candidates contacted by the Research Center, we ultimately chose fifty-three who, like all our other volunteers, were paid a fee.

DEMOGRAPHIC DATA

As noted in chapter 3, the first part of our interview consisted of routine questions about the respondent's age, birthplace, family size, religion, marital and job status. From the data we obtained as a result of these questions (fully supplied in appendix 2), we can extract some general descriptive remarks about the sample and control groups.

Age Distribution. The sex offenders represented all ages, but over 80 percent were between twenty and forty. While the homosexuals tended to be older (about 60% were over thirty), the transsexuals were all under thirty-five. The pornography users ranged between twenty and forty-five. Sixty-five percent of the black low-income sample were under thirty; 59 percent of the black middle-class sample were between twenty-five and thirty-four. The age matching of sex offenders to controls was not particularly accurate, since the control sample contained 22 percent more youths aged twenty to twenty-four than did the sex offender sample. When the sex offenders were subdivided into the rapist and pedophile groups, however, there was an excellent match between the rapists and the controls, although the pedophiles tended to be older.

Birthplace. Excepting the black samples, most members of the other groups were born in the Midwest and Far West, although all areas of the country were represented. Predictably, the black ghetto group contained a high concentration (47%) of individuals born in the Southeast. The black middle-class group included many from the Southwest and a small number (5%) born outside the United States. While most people were born in urban areas, it is surprising to note that 35 percent of the homosexuals and 50 percent of the users began life in a rural environment.

Education. The factor of educational achievement dramatically differentiated the participating subject groups from the controls. Table 3 in appendix 2 reveals that about 54 percent of the sex offenders and 55 percent of the low-income blacks did not complete high school. Neither the rapists nor female object pedophile samples yielded any members who had graduated from college, as compared to 10.8 percent college graduates among the homosexuals and 11 percent among the pornography users. While 41.5 percent of the controls reported partial college experience, only 3.8 percent actually finished college. The socioeconomic status of each group was largely predictable from school background. Of the sex offender group, only 5 percent of the male object pedophiles (perhaps those same 5% who finished college) were members of highly-skilled professions, while 10.8 percent of the homosexuals and 7 percent of the transsexuals so qualified. The user group rated highest in professional credentials, with 30 percent so employed compared to 7 percent of the control group. The black middle-class sample had the highest percent (29.4) in the category of nondegree requiring professions such as salesman and officer manager, although none appeared in the degree-required category. Salary scale naturally coincided with job levels. Twelve percent of the users who came to our attention by answering the flyer we placed in bookstores and theaters reported earning over $20,000 per year. The maximum current salary and best salary ever for all other groups, including controls, did not exceed $15,000 per year except for a few isolated individuals, and 70 percent of all groups except the users earned less than $10,000. The homosexuals, though well educated, did not appear to earn significantly more, but their job descriptions were impressive. When we studied the relationship between salary and job satisfaction, we learned that the rapists most disliked their employment (opinions based on last job prior to institutionalization) but were highly satisfied with their salaries. For homosexuals and transsexuals the reaction was completely reversed. The users, too, liked their jobs but felt their pay was too low, perhaps in comparison with their high educational attainment.

In sum, the statistical matching for all participants in terms of demographic variables was only fair (except for a few specific instances, such as the age of rapists and controls). The rapists differed from controls in present occupational level and degree of satisfaction with best job. The male object pedophiles, significantly older than controls, differed in their range of occupational levels and were more likely to have been raised in some formal religion, predominantly Protestant. The female object pedophiles were also notably older and more likely to be currently married. In general, their educational and occupational levels were low. Thus, we are confident that the subsequently reported differences between rapists and controls do not represent socioeconomic or generational selections. Nevertheless, the differences between the controls and pedophile groups must be scrutinized carefully to take into account the socioeconomic, educational, and generational differences, particularly with regard to the availability of pornography.

The contrasts between homosexuals and controls revealed that the former were older and better educated, on the average, but equal in income. This suggests a degree of underachievement for the homosexual sample. Similarly, the transsexuals had attained higher occupational levels than the controls but were equal in age range, educational level, and income. The users diverged from the controls in containing a higher percentage of respondents around forty to forty-four years old; and users generally had reached a higher occupational level than controls. This suggests that conclusions concerning contrasts between these groups and controls should be interpreted cautiously to determine whether they result from educational, occupational, or generational differences.

I really didn't come across too much
and I'm sorry for it in a way because
my first sex experiences were bad.
I think people should be aware of what sex in life really is.
My first experience with a girl . . .
I didn't know precautions . . . I didn't know about
venereal diseases. . . . I feel that a lack
of knowledge of sex is bad.

FEMALE OBJECT PEDOPHILE

5

FREQUENCY OF EXPOSURE
TO EROTICA IN PREADOLESCENCE,
ADOLESCENCE, AND ADULTHOOD

Perhaps no vision is more disturbing to parents than that of an immature mind encountering erotica and deriving false and disturbing images of adult sexuality. The idea that individuals are particularly influenced by impressions of adult behavior received during the preadolescent and adolescent periods is very popular — and generally valid. As for sexual development, multiple influences within the family, the schools, and the community at large operate concurrently as part of the largely informal sex education perpetuated in our society. What role, if any, does exposure to erotica play in this informal process of sexual education? In this chapter and the ones that follow, we shall attempt to present some evidence, derived from our interviews on this issue.

Our concern here is with the frequency of exposure to erotica during the preadolescent and adolescent periods. In our research, we hoped to determine whether individuals who were exposed to considerable erotica in these formative years were more likely to develop unorthodox sexual tendencies as adults than groups with minimal exposure. Further, we hoped to determine whether exposure to any particular type of erotica was correlated with subsequent sexual attitudes and practices. In later chapters, we will deal not so much with the *frequency* of exposure to erotica as with the impact of specific and highly vivid encounters with an erotic stimulus, in an attempt to determine the effect of these encounters on sexual attitudes and behavior.

Our clinical research interview probed the respondent's exposure and reaction to sexual stimuli during three key time periods: preadolescence (six to ten), adolescence (the teen-age years), and maturity (year prior to questionnaire). Starting with preadolescence, we asked if the respondent had encountered pictures or cartoons of nude people or sex acts, and if so, who had provided them. Did he learn anything about sex from these sources and had he wished to react to the stimulus in a sexual way?

PREADOLESCENCE

Sex Offenders. Approximately one-third of all the sex offender respondents, like the controls, claimed no contact with erotica during preadolescence. About two-thirds of those who did claim contact stated that they were first exposed to erotic material between the ages of nine and twelve; the remaining third first encountered it between ages seven to eight. These ages parallel the data from control groups.

When questioned about the type of erotic stimuli they had seen, 20 percent to 35 percent of the sex offenders and 34 percent of the controls mentioned commercially available photographs from *Playboy* and similar magazines, and nudist camp publications. The source of these photos was usually an unsuspecting parent's bureau drawer or the secret collection of an older sibling. Only the rapist sample dramatically differs here: 30 percent of the rapists, as opposed to 2 percent of the controls, said that they had encountered pornographic photos that displayed explicit sexual acts rather than the less potent homages to nudity that adorn most drugstores.

Respondents were also asked to describe the content and form of erotic stimuli, particularly those details that contributed to the viewer's impression that a sex act rather than simple nudity was being depicted. The following excerpt from this section of an interview reveals that preadolescents are clearly able to distinguish between the two.

RESP.: Probably my first thing like that was some of my father's magazines and paperbacks.

INT.: *When was the first time you saw these magazines?*
RESP.: Age nine or ten.

INT.: *What did you learn from them?*

RESP.: Well, that's a hard question. My parents aren't necessarily . . . they don't hide themselves. So I was accustomed to nude bodies but in a very unsexual type atmosphere. The magazine portrayed a much more sexual-type description, much more arousing than seeing your mother walking around.

While over 90% of the respondents observed nudity at this age, the remembered details are few and hazy except for awareness of the more obvious physical differences between the sexes. The small percentage who had seen pictures of intercourse were largely unable to describe the visual impact of these pictures in any detailed way. This prevalent lack of focus seems to jibe with the respondents' own claim that they learned very little about sex or anatomy from this preadolescent exposure. As one respondent commented: "I was always, at that age, really confused about just what the sex act was and how they went about it." Most early experiences amounted to little more than a furtive peep show, a quick flip of a nude centerfold, or a brief hookup to a smutty conversation. The participant's immaturity as well as the conflicting emotions of curiosity and repugnance caused him to suppress most of the salient details. In the absence of reliable or even recognizable sex information, it seems likely that the resulting imitative sexual behavior was either insignificant or nonexistent, especially since home was probably the setting and friends or siblings the source. Many preadolescents registered the harm caused by their parents' hypocritical attitude toward sex, as something to be hidden in a drawer rather than discussed openly in the living room. "I've always been brought up that sex was dirty, sex was not to be practiced, only by adults, and I think that this is very wrong. And I think this *Playboy* article was proving that sex would be accepted and it isn't a bunch of dirtiness like I had always been told through my life."

Homosexuals and Transsexuals. While 42 percent of the homosexuals and 35 percent of the controls mentioned no preadolescent contact with erotica, the groups matched on choosing the ages nine to twelve as most likely to contain an exposure incident. Only 16 percent of the homosexuals as opposed to 41 percent of the controls, however, mention seeing commercial photographs, and some of these were of the Charles Atlas muscle-flexing type. When these groups were asked about sexual activity following exposure, the frequency of *yes* responses was very low: 25 percent for homosexuals, 12 percent for controls, and 0 percent for transsexuals. Typically, the sexual activity reported was masturbation. Sharp differences emerged between homosexuals and transsexuals when they described their preadolescent companions during erotic exposure. Homosexuals, like controls, were generally with friends or alone, while transsexuals reported being with some family member (29% with a sibling and 43% with other relatives). Thirteen percent of controls reported being with a sibling, none with other relatives.

Twenty-six percent of users and 34 percent of controls reported no exposure at all to erotica during preadolescence, but those users who viewed erotica mentioned the same sources as controls — magazines and photos. Both groups reported viewing depictions of nudity, but users described more frequently (53% vs. 25%, p < .01)* a stimulus in which sexual intercourse was shown. One respondent clearly remembers a silk-screen scroll, probably of Asian origin, which unwound to reveal "a man and a woman in intercourse position. Maybe it showed them in several different positions. But it showed the actual sex act." Another recalled photographs of oral copulation as well as conventional intercourse. "And you know, some pretty far-out stuff like a man after he reached his climax and all the sperm." But such vivid recall of preadolescent events was the exception rather than the rule.

Generally, the context of exposure (other persons present, or the place) did not differ for the two groups. Users reported an age of first exposure to erotica that was significantly younger than controls or any other group. Sixty-one percent of the users reported seven to eight years as the age of first exposure; 32 percent, nine to twelve; while 32 percent and 61 percent of the controls, respectively, reported those ages (p < .05). In addition, 7 percent of users reported less than six years as the age of first exposure, while no respondents in the control group so reported.

Neither group apparently acted out anything of a sexual nature afterward, but there was a trend for controls (35% vs. 9% for users) to have expressed a desire to do so. "I had been curious and wanted to hurry up and grow up." This trend probably relates to the older age of exposure for controls.

Black Samples. In a search for subcultural variations in the experience with erotica, we compared our black and white control samples. Two black samples had been selected, a black low-income sample and a black middle-income sample. The black low-income sample differed sharply from the white controls on a number of levels, while few, if any, differences appeared between black middle-income respondents and white controls.

An equal number of black respondents and controls experienced no

---

* P < .01 indicates the probability that the obtained difference in percents is due to chance. For p < .05 the chance is 5 in 100, for p < .01 the chance is 1 in 100, and for p < .001 the chance is 1 in 1,000 that the obtained difference is due to chance.

erotica during their preadolescent years (34% for both). Of those who did experience erotica, the black low-income group reported significantly *less* exposure to commercial photos of an erotic nature (16% black low income vs. 41% controls, p < .06) and a higher incidence of exposure to pornographic photos (50% black low-income vs. 2% controls, p < .001). Nudity was present in the erotica experienced by both groups, but as might be anticipated from the above data, sex acts were more frequently present in the erotica seen by black low-income respondents (85% vs. 25%, p < .02). One respondent said that in the seventh grade he had seen photos of intercourse and oral-genital lesbian activity.

While the context of the erotic experience was similar for both groups, the age of first exposure was significantly younger for the black low-income group. Twenty-three percent reported less than six years as age of first exposure; 30 percent, seven to eight years; 46 percent, nine to twelve years. This contrasts with control data where 62 percent report nine to twelve; 38 percent, seven to eight; 0 percent, less than six, p < .03.

While both groups seemed to have acquired the same degree of knowledge about human anatomy from these experiences, 21 percent of the black low-income group stated that they had learned something about heterosexual intercourse, as opposed to only 2 percent of the controls (p < .02). And 57 percent of the black low-income sample said that actual sex activity followed the exposure to erotica, compared to 13 percent for the controls. The black middle-income sample differed from controls in revealing a lower frequency of respondents who saw no erotica as preteen-agers (14% black middle-income and 34% controls, p < .10). They also claimed a higher incidence of exposure to pornographic photos (21% vs. 2%, p < .01) and, unlike the black low-income sample, higher exposure to cartoons depicting sexual activity (40% black middle-income vs. 21% controls, p < .001).

Both groups affirm that nudity was present in the stimuli (91% for both), but 68 percent of the black middle-income sample suggested that sex acts were depicted, while only 25 percent of the controls so reported.

There were some differences in the context of exposure. More black middle-income respondents named school as the setting (53.8% vs. 20% controls) while more controls mentioned a home (60% vs. 31% blacks). Along these same lines, the black middle-income participants were more often with a friend during exposure (79% vs. 52% controls), while fewer reported ever being alone (15% vs. 35% controls, p < .09).

Unlike the black low-income sample, the black middle-income sample reported a later age of first exposure (80%, nine to twelve years vs. 62% controls; 20%, seven to eight years vs. 38% controls). Once again, however, more of the black middle-income group reported having learned something about heterosexual intercourse (21% vs. 2% for controls, p < .01). Unlike the black low-income sample, the black middle-income group reported a low incidence of sexual activity subsequent to exposure (14% vs. 13% for controls).

Summary of Preadolescent Data. Generally, the similarities between the groups are more striking than the differences. Certain trends do emerge, however, which are worthy of consideration. While the control samples and various sex varietal groups agreed on frequency of exposures as pre-teen-agers, it appears that controls were more likely to have encountered a sample of nudity while other groups reported a higher frequency of exposure to representations of sexual acts. The frequencies here are not high, nor are all members of the groups involved, but a higher percentage occurred than was true for controls.

There are some suggestions of a unique pattern for transsexuals, in which they describe a younger age of first exposure to erotica, in association with some family member. Whether this exposure represented a purposeful attempt at sex education or some more unusual circumstance is difficult to determine from our data.

It was rare that a respondent in any of the sex deviate groups engaged in actual sexual activity following exposure as a preadolescent. Inadequate knowledge and lack of confidence effectively undermine the youngster's urge to imitate what he thinks he has seen. "I don't know if I actually learned anything other than something like '69.' I think I may have picked up the mutual copulation in pictures. But it seems like everything I learned was from hearsay."

On occasion, however, the manner in which human relationships are portrayed in erotica may have a more serious effect on the formation of early sex attitudes. (Recall Kronhausen's view that this was one basis for distinguishing between pornography and erotic realism in art.)

INT.: *Was there anything you found out about sex that you later learned was not so?*

RESP.: I just got the idea that by seeing these types of things and *Playboy* books and stuff like that that sex was sort of an irresponsible sort of thing. You just do it and get your kicks off and this is it. You know, go around and seduce and all that. Get as much as you can. And I've learned over the years that it's not that kind of a thing. You can't be running around looking for sex all the time.

In the black low-income group we do see reports of sexual activity following exposure to erotica; however, this activity appears to be but one component of socialization in poorer socioeconomic areas of our cities. The claim of these low income respondents that they learned something about heterosexual activity from this preadolescent experience is compatible with other data we gathered connecting the lack of sex education either at home or in school to the loaded role that pornography may play in lower — rather than middle — income environments.

ADOLESCENCE

In this section, we will present data dealing with reports of exposure to various types of pornographic stimuli during the adolescent period. Covering in order photos, films, and books, the respondent was asked whether he had seen a specific stimulus, say a nude female, and if he answered affirmatively, he was asked to estimate the number he had encountered during his adolescent years. These frequency estimates were subdivided into four categories for the purpose of analysis, as follows: (1) never seen; (2) one to ten reported; (3) eleven to fifty reported; and (4) fifty or more reported. Comparisons between groups were carried out, using the chi-square statistic* to determine whether significant differences existed in reports of experience. In this chapter, we present only those figures that indicate the percent of subjects who reported *never* having seen each class of erotic stimuli. Since a high percentage of *never* reports is associated with a low frequency of exposure, in a given sample, the reader can comprehend the trends in the data without having to wade through endless tables.

INSTITUTIONALIZED SEX OFFENDERS

In figure 1, the reports of those who never encountered the various erotic stimuli are presented for the three sex offender samples as contrasted with the controls. We will discuss each group separately.

Rapists. The trend is for a higher frequency of *never* reports for rapists, when compared to controls, across all media and erotic acts. Few significant chi-squares are found, however, and these are for photos of partially and fully nude women and for books describing nudity and oral-genital relations, where the rapist reports significantly less exposure than controls.

---

* This statistic indicates whether the obtained frequencies differ from a distribution of frequencies generated purely by chance. The degree of deviation from the chance distribution is expressed as a probability figure: $p < .05$, $p < .01$, etc.

ADOLESCENT REPORTS OF EXPOSURE TO VARIOUS EROTIC STIMULI
FOR INSTITUTIONALIZED SEX OFFENDERS vs. CONTROLS

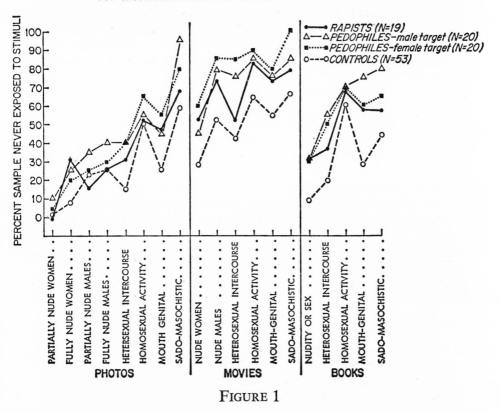

FIGURE 1

Pedophiles — Male Object. Sharper differences between these subjects and controls are suggested by figure 1. Across all stimuli in all three media (photos, movies, and books) more of these pedophiles than of the controls report *never* having encountered these erotic stimuli as adolescents. Significant chi-squares are more numerous than was the case for the rapists. The male object pedophile report significantly less adolescent exposure to photos of partially and fully nude women, heterosexual intercourse and sadomasochistic activity, movies of heterosexual intercourse, and books describing nudity or sex, heterosexual intercourse, oral-genital and sadomasochistic activity.

There is a remarkable correlation between the sexual behavior of pedophiles who select young boys as sexual partners, and the lack of access to symbolic representations of heterosexual intercourse reported during adolescence. This is the one type of stimulus for which significant chi-squares were obtained in all three media. Whether the statistical connection reflects a specific avoidance of this type of erotic stimulus, or the extreme in a total pattern of limited exposure to erotica during adolescence, is difficult to determine from these data. It is interesting to note that these pedophiles, who are homosexuals of a special type, do not differ from controls in reports of exposure to photos or books depicting homosexual activity. They had no greater exposure but a level equal to that of the controls. This suggests that their homosexual interest may have been present to some extent during their adolescent years.

Pedophiles — Female Object. The adolescent data for these child molesters who prefer little girls are very similar to that of the other pedophile group in revealing less exposure to erotic stimuli than controls. Interestingly, as for the other pedophile sample, significant chi-squares are found for representations of sexual intercourse regardless of the media. There are also significant differences for photos representing oral-genital activities, and movies portraying female nudity and sadomasochistic activity. It is clear that the two groups of sex offenders who prefer immature partners report a strikingly low degree of exposure to symbolic depictions of mature and approved sexuality (heterosexual intercourse) during adolescence.

HOMOSEXUALS AND TRANSSEXUALS

Adolescent reports for these two samples are presented in figure 2 below. Here we see even sharper differences from controls than were reported for the institutionalized sex offenders. During teen-age years both homosexuals and transsexuals reported measurably less exposure than controls across all media. The number of significant differences are far greater than the nonsignificant ones. The stimuli on which they do not differ from controls are photos of partially and fully nude males, movies of homosexual acts, and books describing heterosexual intercourse. All but the latter are more likely to interest the homosexually inclined, suggesting that these individuals may have sought out, as adolescents, erotically tinged photos relevant to their emerging homosexual interest.

The data for the transsexuals also indicate less adolescent exposure to erotica than was experienced by the controls. It is worth nothing that transsexuals entered our study because they believed themselves to be of the opposite sex and wished treatment to confirm this role. Yet they report a notably low exposure to stimuli in their teen-age years in which the opposite sex is presented in some sexually provocative way (photos of fully nude women, heterosexual intercourse, and oral-genital relations; books describing nudity or sex, heterosexual and oral-genital relations). Thus, the curiosity and interest in taking on the role of the oppo-

ADOLESCENT REPORTS OF EXPOSURE TO VARIOUS EROTIC STIMULI
FOR HOMOSEXUALS AND TRANSSEXUALS vs. CONTROLS

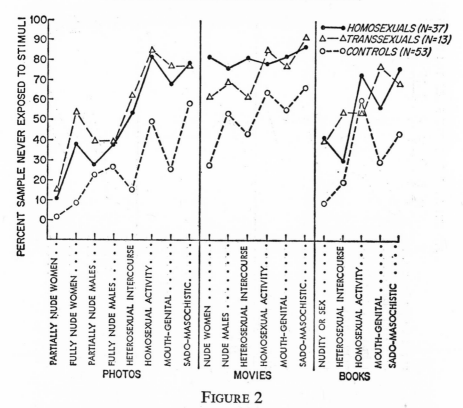

FIGURE 2

site sex did not appear to stimulate them to search out erotica likely to provide information about that sex. More often these respondents related that they found objects associated with the opposite sex (clothing, particularly) to be more erotic than commercially produced pornography.

USERS OF PORNOGRAPHY

As figure 3 illustrates, people who are currently avid buyers and consumers of commercially available pornography indicate an adolescent pattern similar to that of the sex offender and nonheterosexual samples. They report generally less exposure to erotica than controls, and reveal significant differences for photos of fully nude women, fully nude males, and, as has been the case for almost all the noncontrol samples, photos of heterosexual intercourse. In addition, they cite a lower frequency of adolescent exposure for movies of heterosexual intercourse and sado-

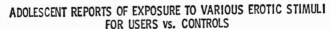

ADOLESCENT REPORTS OF EXPOSURE TO VARIOUS EROTIC STIMULI
FOR USERS vs. CONTROLS

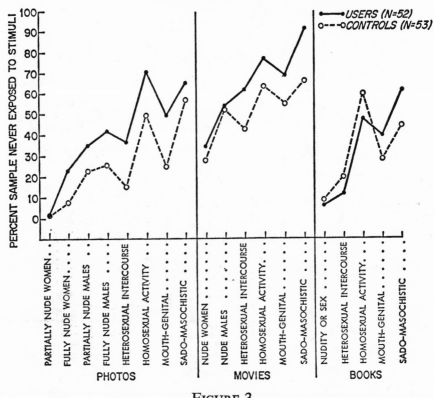

FIGURE 3

masochism. There are, however, few significant differences for erotica
portrayed in books. Generally, the pornography user of today recalls
dramatically little exposure to erotica as a teen-ager, and the most consistent differences from controls occur for stimuli representing heterosexual intercourse.

BLACK CONTROL SAMPLES

The data for the black low-income control sample does not differ
greatly from white controls. There is not a significant chi-square for any
erotic stimuli in any media. This is particularly interesting as the preadolescent data did suggest more intensive exposure to erotica during this
earlier period. Clearly, the groups are more similar as adolescents. Like-
wise, we find few definite gaps between black middle-income and white
controls. There are only two noted chi-squares between this sample and
the white controls, one for books describing nudity or sex and the other

for books describing oral-genital activity. In contrast with the noncontrol samples, all three control samples report very similar degrees of exposure to erotica as teenagers.

RECENT EXPOSURE TO EROTICA

A similar scheme of questioning was used to cover the respondent's exposure to erotica during the year prior to the interview, or, in the case of the sex offenders, the year prior to their institutionalization.

INSTITUTIONALIZED SEX OFFENDERS

Rapists. Once again the rapists report less exposure to pornography for the recent adult period than the controls. In figure 4, we see that significant chi-squares are found for stimuli depicting heterosexual inter-

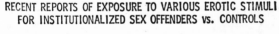

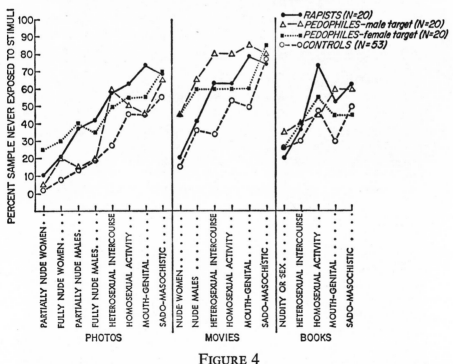

FIGURE 4

course represented in photos and films, and for films containing male nudity and oral-genital relations. The differences between rapists and controls concerning recent experiences are greater than for their adolescent patterns. It is worth noting that once again the rapists may be distinguished from the controls by virtue of their reported underexposure to stimuli representing heterosexual intercourse.

Pedophiles — Male Object. Figure 4 indicates that this sample reports generally less exposure than do the controls for adulthood. The recent data suggest that those pedophiles who prefer little boys do not differ from controls in their reported exposure, in the year prior to institutionalization, to photos of fully and partially nude males, again paralleling their adolescent data. While the male object pedophiles do not differ from controls on stimuli representing male nudity, they do report less exposure to photos depicting true homosexual activity. Since their sexual behavior involves a homosexual interest in immature partners, the selective interest in nudity but avoidance of "true" homosexual erotica seems quite compatible with their sex practices.

Pedophiles — Female Object. Figure 4 indicates that these child molesters who prefer little girls report less exposure to erotica for the year prior to their institutionalization. Once again the data reflect an underexposure to stimuli describing heterosexual intercourse, true for all three sex offender samples in their recent reports.

HOMOSEXUALS AND TRANSSEXUALS

The data for the homosexuals, presented in figure 5, contrasts markedly with their adolescent reports. In almost all media and for all stimuli, the homosexuals report significantly more exposure to erotica than controls. It is a rare erotic stimulus for which they do not show a markedly greater degree of exposure during the year prior to the interview.

As might be expected, the homosexuals register a much higher rate of exposure to homosexual than heterosexual erotica. In contrast with adolescent reports, the adult homosexual, clearly confirmed in his role, actively searches for and uses erotica describing explicit homosexual relations. The very high frequencies of exposure suggest an almost obsessive interest in homosexual erotica, indicating that sexuality is a central concern of this sample of homosexuals.

The same table shows that transsexuals do not report the "crossover" effect from the adolescent data shown by homosexuals. In adulthood, as in adolescence, they mention less exposure to erotica than controls; however, few significant chi-squares are found. There is a trend, of bor-

RECENT REPORTS OF EXPOSURE TO VARIOUS EROTIC STIMULI
FOR HOMOSEXUALS AND TRANSSEXUALS vs. CONTROLS

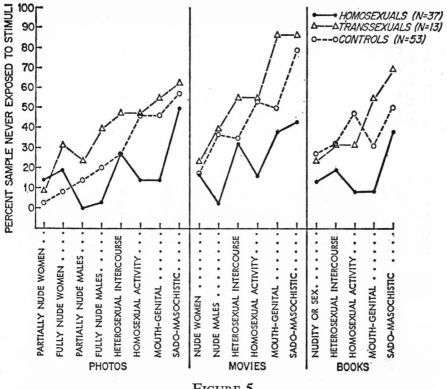

FIGURE 5

derline significance (p < .10), for the transsexuals to report more frequent exposure to books describing homosexuality.

USERS

The current reports for the users resemble the pattern of the homosexual sample to a marked degree. The crossover from significantly low adolescent exposure to significantly increased recent exposure is illustrated in figure 6. The mature user's avid pursuit of pornography in all media suggests a compulsive need to satisfy his previously unfulfilled sexual appetite.

BLACK CONTROL SAMPLES

As with the adolescent data, few important differences emerged between the two black control samples and the white controls. The only category reflecting an appreciable difference between adolescence and

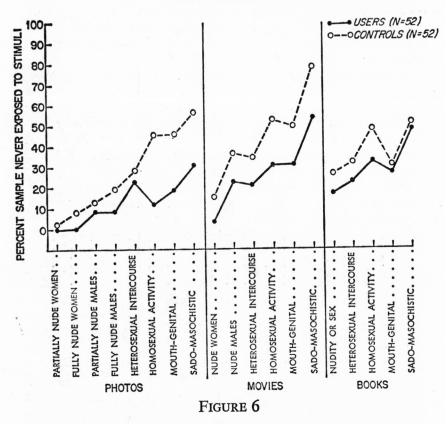

FIGURE 6

maturity was films depicting either nude women or oral-genital relations. The black low-income respondents had seen considerably fewer
— but this statistic may reflect the distance or cost involved in attend-
ing theaters where such films are available, or the total lack of such
theaters in southeastern urban ghettos. And the black middle-income
sample, as compared to the white controls, mentioned seeing more
photos of heterosexual intercourse and reading fewer books describing
oral-genital relations.

SUMMARY AND CONCLUSIONS

In our search for correlations between adult sexual patterns
and reports of frequency of exposure to erotica, the data for preadolescence was largely incidental. Almost all preadolescents have encoun-

tered some form of erotica, which typically portrayed nudity and little else. The erotica was either found around the house, courtesy of a parent's or older sibling's personal possessions, or passed around at school. The one exception was the black low-income sample, which reported that exposure to erotica in preteen years occurred almost exclusively in school.

There are some suggestions in the data that the sex offender groups, particularly the rapists, were exposed as preadolescents to more explicit erotica than the controls. They report a higher frequency of exposure to pictures or books portraying sexual relations. This is the only indication in our data that individuals who developed abnormally in their sexual lives were exposed to more explicit erotica in preadolescent years than individuals who developed normally.

When we examined the reports of frequency of exposure to erotica during adolescence, contrasts between sex offenders, transsexuals, homosexuals, users, and controls were very striking. Most persons in all groups had seen examples of partial nudity as teenagers, and few had seen examples of sadomasochistic activity. Generally, the rapists and the child molesters reported seeing less erotica of all kinds than the controls did. The rapists differed less from controls than did the two pedophile groups, but even here there were significant differences.

The pedophiles had seen less pornography of every kind than had the controls. Only 62 percent of these sex offenders had seen representations of heterosexual intercourse, while 85 percent of the control group had encountered this kind of pornography as teen-agers.

Persons who are avid buyers and consumers of commercial pornography (the user sample) show a pattern closer to the sex offender and nonheterosexual than to the control group. As teen-agers they had seen less pornography of every kind than controls had. This was also true for the homosexuals and, to a lesser extent, the transsexuals. All our non-control groups, then, were markedly lacking in adolescent experience with stimuli that represent the culture's definition of the sex act.

Comparing the sexual behavior patterns for the past year of the various samples with those of adolescence revealed some interesting contrasts. The sex offender samples were generally similar in reporting less recent exposure to erotica than controls. This was also true for the transsexual sample. The homosexuals and users, however, present a striking contrast to their adolescent reports, as they indicate an extremely high degree of current exposure. It appears that both groups developed an obsessive interest in erotica — the homosexuals in homosexual erotica and the users in both heterosexual and homosexual erotica.

The pattern for the homosexuals suggests a high sensitivity to sexual stimuli in general, of which erotica is but one subclass. It is very likely that their marked interest in homosexual erotica reflects an active involvement in the "homosexual community" (Hooker, 1962), as might be expected of a homophile organization of the type from which this sample was selected. Coleman (1972) suggests that "where the homosexual has become affiliated with an organized homosexual group, there is a tendency for him to think of his problems as a group problem. . . . In such cases there may be little feeling of fear or conflict and the individual may accept his homosexual behavior as a perfectly natural form of sexual expression; he may even take pride in his homosexual behavior and consider himself 'emancipated' from conventional heterosexual morality" (p. 485). One way to demonstrate emancipation may be to encounter, as often as possible, homosexual erotica. Since our data are based on a sample of homosexuals willing to join a homophile organization and to be publicly identified as such, it is difficult to know whether these trends also apply to the "silent majority" of homosexuals who do not openly acknowledge their sexual preference.

The users do not ordinarily belong to some organized subculture in society, so it is hard to interpret their behavior on this basis. Clearly, their interest in erotica is compensatory. It is as if they hope to "make up for lost time," for the lack of experience in adolescence.

The fact that all our noncontrol groups, no matter what their age, education, or occupation, reported less exposure to erotica when they were adolescents than did our controls (black or white), suggests that a reasonable exposure to erotica, particularly during adolescence, reflects a high degree of sexual interest and curiosity that coincides with adult patterns of acceptable heterosexual interest and practice. Contrary to our expectations, and those of many popular writers, less-than-average adolescent exposure to pornography reflects either active avoidance of heterosexual stimuli, or limitation to an environment where such materials are unavailable. It appears that the amount of exposure to pornography is a surface manifestation of the total pattern of sexual development. If sexual development proceeds along an unorthodox track, then unorthodox patterns of sexual behavior will result, including either underexposure to pornography or an obsessive interest in it.

So far, we have examined only one facet of the impact of erotica — the frequency of exposure. In the succeeding chapters we shall attempt to go beyond these relatively superficial data to explore the inner experiences of our respondents when they encountered particularly meaningful erotica. In this way, we hope to understand the impact of erotica on sexual feelings, sexual attitudes, and the overt behavior of our respondents.

6

PEAK ADOLESCENT EXPERIENCE
WITH EROTICA: SEX OFFENDERS

Frequency of exposure is but one index of the intensity of an individual's experience with erotica. Often, single encounters with a picture, book, or film of an erotic nature are so emotionally arousing, either positively or negatively, that the feelings and images persist in the consciousness for months or years. The images may constitute an unwelcome intrusion, or may be actively encouraged, for the pleasurable stimulation that results. Almost everyone can recall a cartoon book passed around in school, a photo usually in poor focus, or an erotic film seen in adolescence. In fact, in order to appreciate more readily the significance of the data reported in this chapter, the reader may wish to duplicate the mental set of the participants in the study.

Think back over your teen-age years, and try to recall everything erotic that you encountered in printed form, in photos, and in films. Now that your memory is focused on that subject, think of the piece of erotica that really *stands out* in your mind. Ordinarily, some image or experience will come immediately to mind, almost as if a television picture had been turned on. Keeping that image in mind will help you understand the logic behind both our questions and our method of coding

71

the answers for statistical analysis. The formal outline of the questions is included in the interview form, questions 76–127 (appendix 1).

In this chapter, we examine the reactions of the institutionalized sex offenders to those experiences they recalled as their most vivid encounters with erotica during adolescence. We are concerned with their immediate response to the stimulus, as they remembered it; the nature of the sexual activities they wished to and/or actually did pursue after the experience; and the influence of the experience on their attitudes toward sexuality. In the next chapter, we shall present the same data for the homosexuals, transsexuals, and users. As in chapter 5, all statistics will be contrasted with the reports of the control sample.

Nature of peak experiences described. Each respondent was asked to specify the most vivid encounter with an erotic experience during adolescence. The type of stimulus (photo, book, or movie) and whether it was commercially available (coded pornographic vs. commercial) were determined. For example, 50 percent of the rapists and 50 percent of the male object pedophiles chose some kind of photo as most vivid, as contrasted with 13 percent of the controls ($p < .05$). In the rapist sample, the photo was more likely (35%) to be identified as pornographic while a similar number of male object pedophile respondents identified a commercially available photo.

As for subject matter, the responses of the sex offenders, in particular, ran the gamut of every imaginable (and included some that were less imaginable) type of erotic stimuli. While for some the most highly charged recollection was thumb tripping through *Playboy* — "It was the object of my desire . . . intercourse with a woman like that," for others the material was more explicit — perhaps a series of photos showing intercourse: "They were real specific like showing her thighs and his penis in her." One respondent, a pedophile, gave this unusually long and vividly detailed answer to the question, "What about your peak erotic experience [a book containing sex and violence] makes it stand out in your mind so strongly?"

This guy was a roughneck. I guess that's why I kinda picked up on it because I like workin' around oil fields myself. He was a pretty wild S.O.B., did pretty much what he wanted to do. He made good money, and he lived not just for long term, but each day he had a hell of a time. And he met this girl in this bar and they was makin' out. He was buying her booze and stuff. And finally he asked her did she have a place to stay and she said "Sure, I have a hotel." So they got 'em a bottle and pranced out and went on up to this hotel. . . . She puts some records on and they had soft music and lights turned down low and get the whole scene set up. And he starts makin' out and first thing you know they're sprawled out on the couch and he's having a ball. There was no conversation, they just sorta dropped it until a few minutes later when the act is over. Then she wants to be satisfied. So she suggests to him that he take a wet towel. And he just popped her with it. No place in particular. And she's on the floor and he's popping the hell out of her with that towel. And she's running all over the house hollering, "Hit me, baby, hit me. Make it good to me." To me it was weird as hell. And I guess that's why it sticks out. It strikes me as being weird.

Such total recall confirms the vividness of these peak experiences and the ease with which some respondents could retrieve the details many years later.

Female object pedophiles stand out from all groups as containing the highest percentage (20%, $p < .05$ vs. controls) who could recall no vivid experience with erotica during teen-age years. Twenty-eight percent of the controls, however, mentioned a pornographic film as most vivid. Since this type of erotic stimulus is the most direct representation of sexuality available, the trend is for the controls to report a more explicit erotic stimulus than all sex offender groups (controls, $p < .05$ vs. all sex offender groups).

Age at which peak experience was identified. Each respondent recalled how old he was at the time of this most vivid experience. In table 6 the figures for the three sex offender groups and controls are presented. Only the rapists stand out in reporting a significantly earlier age of peak experience, the average being between thirteen and fifteen years of age. All other samples identify an experience as having occurred in the sixteen to eighteen year period. For rapists, then, the most vivid experience was usually a photo seen early in adolescence. For the controls, the experience was a pornographic movie seen in late adolescence.

Table 6

REPORTED AGES OF INSTITUTIONALIZED SEX OFFENDERS AND CONTROLS
AT THE TIME OF PEAK ADOLESCENT EXPERIENCE WITH EROTICA

	Age			
Subjects	10–12 (%)	13–15 (%)	16–18 (%)	p vs. Controls
Rapists	10	65	25	.001
Male object pedophiles	10	27	63	—
Female object pedophiles	6	27	67	—
Controls	8	19	73	—

Emotions during peak experience. Almost all respondents reported sexual arousal in response to the peak erotic experience. "To me, the act of intercourse itself [as described in the novel *Candy*] was exciting." Or "The girl was pretty nice. And she was goin' for it." Very frequently the mere fact that certain entrenched curiosities were satisfied made the experience a "peak" one. "It was the kinda off-beat type thing. It was the strangeness of it more than anything." In addition, respondents were queried about other emotional reactions to this most vivid sample of erotica, particularly amusement, shame, or disgust. Only 47 percent of the controls reported either shame or disgust as a side effect of this peak experience as opposed to 60 percent of rapists, 80 percent of male object pedophiles, and 81 percent of female object pedophiles. One noncontrol subject reported:

When I read this, I felt like I was sneaky and cheap, really. Usually I'm quite open about what I read and I wasn't then. I guess I could call it frustrating because I did do it and it made me feel like some sort of sneak, or thief, or whatever else you'd want to call it — and I didn't like that feeling.

Guilt was sometimes accompanied by low self-esteem. "I think maybe I kinda felt like maybe I was inferior or something when I saw the way the guy ejaculated because it was unbelievable. . . . I just never came nowhere near that."

These data indicate the sex offenders experienced more conflicting emotions — reporting both arousal and disgust — during this most vivid experience with erotica than controls, precisely the pattern found by Mosher (see chap. 2) for male college students with high sex guilt. This conflict can clearly be detected in the responses of one subject who was shocked by details such as "watching the guy ejaculate and the girl lickin' it" but also stated that the girl's enthusiasm was the most sexually exciting factor in the experience.

The context of the experience. A substantial number of respondents indicated that they were with others, usually friends, at the time of this vivid experience. When asked how the reactions of their peers affected their own feelings concerning the erotic stimulus, noticeable group differences appeared. Table 7 shows that while the controls were largely unaffected by friends' reactions, a small percent found their reactions enhanced by the presence of others. The rapists and male object pedophiles, however, registered a high degree of sensitivity to the reactions of peers. In both groups, a bimodality appears, with substantial numbers of rapists and male object pedophiles reporting inhibition or enhancement due to peers (these two groups are the only ones reporting inhibition of their reaction by peers).

Table 7

REPORTED IMPACT OF FRIENDS' REACTION
TO EROTICA ON THE RESPONDENT
(Percent of Individuals)

Subjects	Inhibited Me	No Effect	Enhanced My Reaction	p vs. Controls
Rapists	36	18	45	.0001
Male object pedophiles	22	33	44	.01
Female object pedophiles	0	50	50	—
Controls	0	78	21	—

Respondents were also asked whether there was anything displayed or described in the erotic stimulus which they had never seen or heard of before. Twenty percent of the male object pedophile group stated that it was the first time that they had seen *full female nudity* (p < .04 vs. controls). The rapists (45% vs. 8% controls) recall this experience as the first time they saw a representation of heterosexual intercourse (p < .02 vs. controls): "I learned how to have sexual intercourse." "I learned all the different types and ways of performing sex." "I learned some of the emotions involved in the sexual act." Twenty percent of the male object pedophile group admitted that the experience constituted their first exposure to homosexual relations.

Aftereffects of peak erotic stimulus. Respondents were asked whether they thought much about this peak erotic experience in the days and weeks afterward. A high percentage of all groups did: rapists, 90 percent; male object pedophiles, 68 percent; female object pedophiles, 85 percent; and controls, 79 percent. When asked whether they wished to try anything portrayed or described in this erotica at a later time, at least 50 percent in each group answered affirmatively (male object pedophiles, 60%, female object pedophiles, 59%; controls, 51%). Only the rapists stand out from all other groups at a statistically significant level p < .01) in containing a higher percentage (88%) who wished to imitate some aspect of sexual activity portrayed in this sample of erotica.

Our interview attempted to pinpoint what component of the erotica respondents desired to imitate. Again, as in type of erotic stimulus deemed most vivid, there was great variation: from having relations with two lesbians simultaneously to "playing rough" with a sex partner; from fellatio to conventional intercourse. All samples except the male object pedophile group stated a desire for some type of heterosexual activity, while the latter included 22 percent who wanted to imitate some type of homosexual activity. No other sample could make this claim. The 68 percent of the male object pedophile group who did *not* desire homosexual activity recalled desires for the same type of heterosexual relations expressed by the other groups. "I wanted to have a woman but there just wasn't one available." "Well, I thought I'd like to have a girl do what she [heroine in book] did to this other man . . . turning him on all over and exploring his body."

Did the respondents actually try out some of the sexual behavior portrayed in their peak erotica? By and large they report that they did, and the figures for male object pedophiles, female object pedophiles, and controls (77%, 87%, and 87%, respectively) did not differ significantly. The rapists, however, had the lowest percent (57%) that attempted to imitate some feature of this peak erotic stimulus ($p < .10$ vs. other groups). Their high-interest statements contrast sharply with low-beam performance. When we asked the nonimitating respondents what had prevented them from accomplishing their erotic goals, the most common answers were lack of an available sex partner, fear of pregnancy, or fear of sex. (Among rapists, these replies were less common — only 15% gave these reasons.)

Theories about the effects of pornography often imply that sexual arousal will be followed immediately by sexual activity. In our interview, the respondents who indicated subsequent imitation were asked when in time had it occurred. As table 8 indicates, few, if any, respondents reported that imitative activity occurred right away (moments, hours, or up to a day later). They were equally divided between those who participated shortly after (days, weeks later) and those who did so months or years later. Thus, the impact of erotica during teen-

Table 8

RESPONDENTS WHO REPORTED SUBSEQUENT IMITATION
OF EROTICA AND TIME OF IMITATION

		Number of Individuals		
Respondents	*Percent Reporting*	*Right Away*	*Shortly After*	*Months-Years After*
Rapists	57	12	63	25
Male object pedophiles	77	10	40	50
Female object pedophiles	87	0	57	43
Controls	85	16	53	31

age years, as reported by our samples, was likely to be a delayed rather than an instantaneous result.

Type of sexual activity desired following peak experience. Erotic pictures or books may awaken in an individual the appetite for a specific sexual act or technique that attracts him by its unexpected novelty or curiosity. Erotica, however, can also trigger a general but intense feeling of arousal which eventually instigates sexual desires not depicted in the original source. Respondents, therefore, were asked what type of sexual activity they felt like engaging in after this most vivid erotic experience. Table 9 shows the percent of respondents in each group who did express sexual desire, broken down by the form of the sexual activity described. This table clearly shows that the rapists, controls, and to a lesser extent the female object pedophile group affirm a desire for some form of heterosexual intercourse. Few respondents in any group wanted homosexual relations. Both pedophile groups, however, in contrast with the rapists and controls, have a significantly higher percentage of other coded responses. When we examined the taped responses, we found that the majority of male object pedophile respondents report masturbation as their desired sex activity, with a few mentioning sadomasochistic activity. In the case of the female object pedophiles, the replies also referred to masturbation, but more often to "any type of sexual activity." Thus, the two child-molester groups apparently desired a less mature form of sexual gratification than the rapists and controls. Possibly, this relates in some fashion to their adult choice of immature sexual partners.

General reactions to erotica during adolescence. We were interested in determining how frequently our respondents experienced the type of erotica they identified as most vivid throughout their adolescent years.

Table 9

PERCENT OF SUBJECTS REPORTING SEXUAL DESIRE FOLLOWING PEAK EROTIC
EXPERIENCE, DIVIDED ACCORDING TO DESIRED SEXUAL ACTIVITY

Subjects	Heterosexual Intercourse	Homosexual Relations	Other	p vs. Control
Rapists	80	0	20	—
Male object pedophiles	50	7	43	.02
Female object pedophiles	64	0	36	.20
Controls	86	0	14	—

Table 10

FREQUENCY OF EXPOSURE DURING ADOLESCENT YEARS TO EROTIC
STIMULI SIMILAR TO THOSE MENTIONED AS MOST VIVID

Subjects	Once	Few Times	Many Times	p vs. Control
Rapists	10	40	50	.05
Male object pedophiles	21	53	26	—
Female object pedophiles	19	50	31	—
Controls	13	65	20	—

In table 10, the frequency estimates offered by the subjects are presented. Only the rapists stand out from the other groups in reporting
more frequent exposure to the kinds of erotic stimuli they identified as
most vivid during adolescence. These data do not contradict the data
presented in chapter 5 concerning the frequency of exposure to erotica
during adolescence. The rapists only report more frequent exposure
than controls for the *most vivid* stimulus — likely to be a photo of some
sort — experienced at a younger age than all other groups. Thus, the
rapists had more years to reexperience this type of stimulus than those
in the other samples. Still, there is a suggestion in these data that the
rapists developed a stronger interest in erotica, at least of a specific type,
than any of the other groups.

Incorporation of erotica into sexual daydreams. Each respondent was
asked how often he thought about sex during his teen-age years. The
modal reply was coded a "good part of the time," which was true for
65 percent of the rapists, 63 percent of pedophiles, female object, and
78 percent of controls, who did not differ significantly. Only 37 percent
of the pedophiles, male object, however, gave this reply. The balance
of the sample was at opposite ends of the sex preoccupation scale, with
26 percent reporting "almost never" and 37 percent who constantly
thought of sex. These figures suggest the possibility that the pedophiles,
male object, include two subsamples of adolescent sexual adjustment:
one very repressed and inhibited, the other obsessively preoccupied with
sex.

In attempting to pinpoint the impact of erotica on recurring sexual
daydreams, the respondents were asked whether scenes from erotica
became part of their regular daydreams. "I could just see myself with
this teen-age girl that I was going with at the time. And the two of us
playing the part in the book." "I was impressed by the pictures I saw,

especially the women. I knew that there was a nice-looking woman out there. And I was gonna get me one. And in the movies where the old hero ends up with the pretty girl. So, you know, I wanted to be a hero." Once again pedophiles, male and female object, and controls did not differ: approximately 65 percent of each group answered affirmatively. However, 95 percent of the rapists (p < .03 vs. all other groups) reported that erotica had an impact on their sex daydreams. These data are quite in keeping with data reported earlier in this chapter concerning the desire to imitate erotica following the most vivid experience.

Along these same lines, the rapists were more likely to report that their recurring sex daydreams incorporated aspects of sexual technique (p < .005 vs. all other groups) or characters (p < .11 vs. all other groups) expressed in erotica they had encountered. "Well, the movie that I saw was kind of a way to show me how to go about a sex act. And the pictures. They were kind of stimulating to see . . . a woman with no clothes on. And I figured, well, that's the way you have to go about it — get her undressed." Or, "Just positions, different positions. I saw them dog-fashion and I picked up on that. Male-female intercourse where the male's behind her goin' in through the rear."

Relationship to masturbation. We asked our respondents about how often they masturbated during their teen-age years. For a contrast, they were then asked how often thoughts of previously encountered erotica stimulated them to masturbate. The rapists overshadow all other groups in relating daily masturbation to thoughts of erotica; however, they also report a generally high rate of masturbation. Pedophiles, male object, show a bimodal tendency, as suggested earlier, in which one quarter of the sample reports never masturbating and one quarter reports daily masturbation. This is congruent with our data suggesting at least two very different sexual histories in this sample.

SUMMARY OF REACTIONS TO MOST VIVID ENCOUNTER WITH EROTICA

Rapists. The rapists mentioned an earlier age of exposure to a relatively mild erotic stimulus (a photo) that aroused them but at the same time disgusted them. While noting an intense desire to imitate the activities shown, only rarely did they satisfy it. Thus, these data reveal them as highly stimulated, tending to repeat contact with the type of erotic stimulus they found most vivid, desiring more mature sexual experiences but frustrated by lack of sex partners or their fear of sex. They relied heavily on masturbation, often stimulated by images garnered from erotica, as a sexual outlet during teen-age years. Generally, the adolescent data suggest high sexual desire, but marked guilt and frustration in realizing mature sexual outlets.

The following excerpts from an interview with a rapist reinforce our conclusions from the statistical data. This respondent had received little or no preadolescent sex education. "I was always about that age really confused just what the sex act was and how they went about it." In adolescence he came across a cartoon booklet. "It showed the man with the great huge penis. I can vaguely remember the gal in it was a prostitute. And the men were all lining up on payday. Then it showed pictures of the actual sex act and him inserting his penis in her and things of that nature." This cartoon book was chosen as the key erotic experience of his adolescent years. In answer to the question, "What makes it stand out in your mind so strongly?" respondent replied, "I think the fact that it gave me a low opinion of women and that there are women like that."

He was then asked to describe the experience in a more detailed way. "I can remember a bunch of men coming home from a factory or mine or something. And they had their paychecks and here was this gal that was a prostitute. And they were all lining up taking their turns. Saying, 'Oh, this was great,' or something. And she was holding the money and really digging it." To the question, "What about it was sexually exciting?" he answered, "Just showing the sex act. The gal really delighted in it. The description of her really digging it."

When we asked this respondent what picture, film, or book had most disgusted him as an adolescent, he countered with a deeply felt experience of his own. "When I was about eleven I had a paper route and I can remember that I was out collecting one day and I came across, you know, beside the road, a condom that had been used. I kinda knew what it was for and everything and what must have taken place, and I pictured in my mind some guy out in the car with a woman and having sex and that was what it was for. And it kinda disgusted me." "Why?" "I don't know. Just being out like that, I guess. I figured it should've been at home, in a home, in bed. Not in a car like that."

We inquired whether other things such as clothes or objects had turned him on. He replied, "I was really curious what a woman looked like. I tried peepin' on my sister one time when she was taking a bath. I tried to go down and watch a neighbor lady one time undress. I didn't want to hang around because I was scared, so I never really saw anything." In this excerpt, we see the rapist's minimal exposure to erotica during preadolescence and adolescence, his intense sexual curiosity, the barriers to satisfying it, and the guilt that accompanied any attempt, whether open or covert, to gratify it.

Pedophiles. These two groups report a peak experience with erotica which occurred mostly during late adolescence, and involved a less explicit stimulus than that reported by controls. They registered sexual arousal, but, like the rapists, alternating with shame and disgust. They were not as desirous as the rapists of imitating sexual behavior depicted in the erotic stimulus, but of those who were so inclined, a high percentage ultimately acted out the desired experience. As with the rapists, the imitation rarely occurred immediately after exposure to erotica, but rather after the passage of substantial periods of time.

The following section of an interview with a female object pedophile is fairly representative. For his key erotic experience, this respondent mentioned a scene in a book. "I think when he was describing the way that he made this girl. And the intercourse he had with her." In answer to what was so memorable about this scene, he said, "Well, he had her on a rooftop. And he was describing her body. How soft it felt. And how full her tits were. Then he went down to her virginia [sic] and he said that the hair around it and so forth and so on." Another question probed what was sexually exciting about this experience. "I think just the way it described the relations between a boy and girl."

There were, however, accompanying negative reactions. "I felt that it was a dirty book and I shouldn't be reading it but yet the more I read the more I wanted to read." The interviewer attempted to isolate the "disgusting" components from the pleasurable ones, but this pedophile could not exactly specify. "Now that I look back on it, I think that the whole book was strictly a disgusting book, but at the time I really enjoyed reading it." One aspect of the book angered him. "I believe the way that they were interrupted or the way that he actually treated the girl after he got what he wanted. He slapped her around. It was basically the roughness about it." Did anything shock him? "The actual sexual intercourse. I was very naïve about these things." Had he learned anything about sex from this experience? "I don't think I really learned anything from the book. I knew practically everything that the book described. I think it was just the idea of reading the book and getting the stimulation from the reading." The respondent said that certain specific scenes from this book merged with his fantasies. "Well, I could just see myself with this teen-age girl that I was going with at the time. And the two of us playing this part in the book."

This excerpt also illustrates the typical naïveté of the female object pedophiles: their curiosity about sex and the guilt that they experienced upon seeing erotica as a teen-ager. It also illustrates the desire to imitate aspects of sexual behavior portrayed in the erotica, and (though not specifically mentioned here) the fact that these fantasies were rarely acted out with real sexual partners.

Certain differences between pedophiles, male and female object, emerged in these adolescent data. First, the female object group had the highest percentage of respondents who reported no peak experience with erotica during their teen-age years. Of those who did, it was most likely to occur during late adolescence. That group also reported significantly less likelihood of imitating activities depicted in erotica right away. Often months or years would go by before they would try the desired sexual behavior.

The male object group stands out from all other examples in its percentage stimulated to try homosexual relations following exposure to erotica. Also, there are notable bimodal trends in this, suggesting division into two groups, one with minimal exposure to erotica during teen-age years and limited sexual experience, and another obsessively preoccupied with sexuality. Both groups appear fixated and have immature sexual patterns — a substantial number reported masturbation as the most desired sexual activity. These same respondents also reported "fear of sex" as the main barrier to seeking more mature sexual outlets.

Generally, the adolescent peak experience data contrasting the sex offenders with controls suggest that all groups were stimulated by this vivid erotic stimulus, but that the sex offenders experienced the high sex guilt pattern demonstrated by Mosher (1970) in which disgust accompanied arousal. The sexual activity desired following this peak experience was most often heterosexual intercourse; typically, however, the groups substituted masturbation. Significant differences appeared in the response patterns of the rapists, as contrasted with the other sex offender groups. The former were fixated on rather simple erotica (a photo) seen at an early age; and they continued to seek out erotic photos throughout adolescence. Highly stimulated but fearful of expressing their sexual desires overtly, they were least likely to attempt imitation of the desired activity. Despite this inhibition, components of the peak erotic stimulus were likely to become part of their regular fantasy life, which was highly focused upon sexuality. The rapists' rate of masturbation during adolescence is also commensurate with this marked level of sexual interest.

This pattern is quite different from that reported for the pedophiles, male object, who evidence less interest in erotica and less preoccupation with sexual fantasies in their reports on adolescence.

7

PEAK ADOLESCENT EXPERIENCE
WITH EROTICA: HOMOSEXUALS,
TRANSSEXUALS, USERS

In chapter 6 we presented data contrasting the three groups of institutionalized sex offenders with the controls on their reactions to their most vivid encounters with erotica during the teen-age years. Here we will present similar data concerning people who lead unusual sexual lives, but who have not been in any significant trouble with the law. All these groups (homosexuals, transsexuals, and users) reported very limited exposure to erotica in their adolescent years. Therefore we are particularly interested in the nature of the peak experience identified (if any) and its impact upon their behavior.

Nature of peak stimulus. As with the institutionalized sex offenders, these groups mentioned photos most often as their most vivid erotic stimulus. "It was the first time I saw *anything* like that and I really do remember seeing the genital contact with both partners." (Seventeen percent of the homosexuals reported seeing a commercially available photo, as did 18 percent of the users; 24 percent of the users had seen a pornographic or "hard-core" photo.) "The woman is in the middle,

83

getting it from both ways; it's a clear picture and you can see they've both got it in her." The transsexuals did not stand out on this index. Also (as with the sex offender sample) both homosexuals and transsexuals are less likely to report a pornographic film as their peak experience (p < .005). This trend can be seen even more clearly in replies to a question asked in the latter part of this section of the interview. Here respondents identified the most sexually exciting stimulus seen during adolescence. These data are presented in table 11.

In table 11 it is clear that the homosexuals and transsexuals are considerably more inclined than the controls to identify a photo, as opposed to a film, as most erotically stimulating during adolescence. (Given the data in chapter 5, indicating that these groups had very limited experience with erotica, they probably never encountered such films.) The group identified as heavy users of pornography did not differ from the controls.

Those homosexuals who listed books as the most vivid stimulus were attracted initially by curiosity, and eventually satisfied if concrete details were supplied. "It was really the very first time I had encountered such a book that really got down to the nitty-gritties." For some the experience was highly educational. "All of a sudden I came to the word *homosexual* and the explanation and after *seventeen* years I said, 'Oh, I see what the problem is.'" A few indulged but were guided by common sense. "Any book with sex in it I get turned on to a certain point. But as far as actually having sex, I didn't need books or anything else to turn me on."

That the stimulus and the age of the experience are linked can be seen in the answers to the next question, concerning the respondent's age at the time of this peak experience. These ages are presented in table 12. As with the institutionalized sex offenders, the controls report a peak experience in late adolescence (sixteen to eighteen) while the

Table 11

MOST SEXUALLY EXCITING STIMULUS

DURING ADOLESCENCE (MEDIA)

Subjects	Printed Material (%)	Photo (%)	Movie (%)	p vs. Control
Homosexuals	17	70	13	.02
Transsexuals	40	60	0	.10
Users	34	42	24	—
Controls	41	31	28	—

Table 12

AGE OF EXPOSURE TO PEAK EROTIC STIMULUS

Subjects	10–12 Years (%)	13–15 Years (%)	16–18 Years (%)	p vs. Control
Homosexuals	7	45	48	.07
Transsexuals	8	53	39	.05
Users	9	40	51	.09
Controls	8	19	73	—

other groups contain a higher percentage locating their peak experience during early adolescence (thirteen to fifteen).

Emotions elicited by stimulus. Generally, all groups report being sexually aroused by this peak erotic stimulus. "Well, I was excited by the male in the picture, mostly." "The boy who was kneeling on the floor, he was masturbating himself and that excited me." Or, "I guess from a voyeuristic standpoint, it aroused me." "Well, I'll put it this way — the undressing, the caressing, and the actual sex is something beautiful." In addition, they were asked whether other emotions, either positive or negative, accompanied the arousal. These were subdivided into positive reactions such as curiosity ("The descriptions . . . were very much down to the detail of the pubic hair.") or envy ("I always wanted to do that. And these boys shown in this picture were very handsome, very beautiful."). There were also the inevitable negative reactions, shame, guilt, and disgust. "Oh yes, it's a little bit of a cross between disgust and anger. The guy kept his socks on and this seemed ridiculous to me." "It was unbelievable that people would do these things." "I thought the women were trashy, low-down and scummy because that's what I had been taught."

Table 13 illustrates the percent of respondents in each group who report negative feelings accompanying this most vivid experience with erotica. Both the homosexuals and the users report significantly more

Table 13

EMOTIONS ELICITED BY PEAK EROTIC STIMULUS

(OTHER THAN AROUSAL)

Subjects	Amusement/ Curiosity (%)	Shame/ Disgust (%)	p vs. Control
Homosexuals	9	91	.04
Transsexuals	40	60	—
Users	21	79	.06
Controls	52	48	—

often the correlated emotions of shame, disgust, or guilt. In fact, in the homosexual sample, this was true of almost all respondents. When the actual reactions of the users were scrutinized, however, we tended to find *guilt* more often than *disgust*. We also learned that the expression of negative emotions accompanying sexual arousal is not related to the age at which the experience occurred. The users, who report significant negative feelings associated with this peak erotic experience, particularly guilt, mention as many late adolescent experiences as controls. The homosexuals, who affirm an earlier age of experience, also admit more negative emotions. The transsexuals, while claiming an earlier experience, state no more negative feelings than do controls. Thus, the appearance of negative feelings relates to other variables than the age of exposure.

Context of peak experience. Generally, most respondents reported being with someone at the time of this peak experience, typically friends or a relative of about the same age. One respondent accurately summed up the appeal of spectatorship. "I guess it was a feeling of being in the room and yet not having the nervousness of being a participant. It was as though I wasn't called upon to act, no one was looking at me, but I was still close enough to the subject where I could learn something and I could see, of course, a female, and, generally speaking, they were fairly goodlooking. The much better looking the more excited I got, of course. But I think it was that feeling of remaining separate and yet still enjoying." When asked how the companion's reaction affected their own, only the transsexuals stand out from the controls (p < .05) in that a substantial minority (25% vs. 0% controls) reported being inhibited by presence of other people. The homosexuals rather than controls tended to report enhancement of reaction by peers (40% homosexuals vs. 21% controls, p < .10).

When the respondents were asked whether the erotic stimulus included anything that they had never seen or heard of before, several trends emerged. While it seems fairly reasonable that a sixteen-year-old might not have observed oral or anal sex or even a "live show" depicting standard intercourse, such comments as, "I didn't know women had hair down there; I had never seen a woman's breasts exposed" or "It was the first time I had a good close look at a woman's organs" reveal that for many individuals basic knowledge of sex before this peak experience is often nonexistent. Eleven percent of the homosexuals and 12 percent of the users reported that it was the first time that they had seen a fully nude female (p < .10 vs. controls). Notable also was the fact that only 11 percent of the homosexuals indicated that this peak experience represented the first time that they had seen homosexuality represented.

It should also be kept in mind that only 20 percent of the homosexuals selected as their most vivid erotic stimulus one depicting homosexuality. Thus, the average homosexual's exposure to homosexual erotica either occurred later in life, or was not one of the most vivid experiences in his teen-age years.

As with other groups, we asked whether anything new about sex was learned from this peak experience. Once again, a varied spectrum is evident in the replies. "I wasn't really conscious of learning anything." "Nothing except knowledge of anatomy." "Well, about the way that male and female animal life carries on. . . . Course I'd seen breeding on the farm." "My first . . . understanding of male oral or anal contact." "I learned to enjoy fellatio. That's what I learned." And in this era of spirited assault on male chauvinism, "I learned that women actually enjoy sex." The transsexuals and users stand out from controls (p < .02 transsexuals, p < .05 users vs. controls) in containing a higher percentage of respondents who claim to have learned how to have heterosexual relations from the erotic stimulus (29% of transsexuals and 20% of the users reporting affirmatively): "I had my ideas of intercourse confirmed." There were no other group differences for other types of sex (oral-genital, homosexual, sadomasochistic).

Subsequent reactions to peak experiences. In this section of the interview, we asked about the short- and long-term impact of this peak experience on the respondent's sexual development. When we inquired whether they thought about the contents of the erotic stimulus later on, in all groups but the transsexuals at least 80 percent replied affirmatively, while only 54 percent of the transsexuals did so, a significantly lower percentage (p < .05). When asked whether they wished to try any activity shown in the erotica at a later date, approximately half the subjects in each group responded affirmatively. "I wanted to get a full climax. One that would absolutely leave her, as this girl was [in the erotic material] a throbbing, soaking mess, just lying there half-dead. And I thought this would be very nice." Or, "I wanted to try all of it but the whipping." "I wanted to go down on a woman after I had seen it done." "I wanted to try new positions." "I wanted to try everything." Once again, a lower percentage of transsexuals (30%) and a slightly higher percentage of users (68%) answered yes. These percents do not differ significantly from the controls, however.

Of the respondents who wished to try some aspect of the sexual behavior characterized as most vivid, a certain number actually did so. Table 14 indicates the number of respondents who claimed to desire this sort of imitation, the number who actually carried it out, and when they did so. Since some of the numbers are small, it was felt that the

Table 14

NUMBERS DESIRING IMITATION OF ACTIVITY PORTRAYED IN PEAK
EROTIC STIMULUS AND TIME ELAPSED BEFORE IMITATION

Subjects	Number Desiring Imitation	Number Actually Imitating	When Imitation Occurred		
			Right Away	Weeks Later	Months or Years Later
Homosexuals	14	10	1	4	5
Transsexuals	4	2	0	2	0
Users	33	23	5	10	8
Controls	22	19	3	10	6

actual frequencies rather than percentages would be more easily understood.

The data in the left-hand column are those discussed in the previous paragraph, represented here in frequency form. Of the fourteen homosexuals who wanted to imitate the activity the stimulus portrayed, ten actually did so, typically some months or years later. "I didn't try it in relation to the book. It came about on its own natural course, had I not even read the book." "Well, I tried it with a boy first, but that was later on." Only a few of the transsexuals actually wanted to copy the activity in the erotic stimulus, as noted above, and half of this small number actually did attempt to imitate this behavior shortly afterward. In the user sample, two-thirds of those who wanted to imitate the stimulus did so, usually some time after the experience of exposure. The controls have the highest frequency of actual imitation, again some time after the exposure. "I think I tried everything that was shown." "Going down on a woman; I liked it after I tried it."

In general our respondent groups did not participate in immediate imitation of erotic scenes for various reasons. "I usually masturbated; I always wished there was a girl present." "I would have liked to go and get a girl and go to bed; I didn't because I didn't know any." If it occurred at all, such modeling followed some time after the experience, and often months or years later. In these cases, it was very hard to attribute the activity to this earlier vivid experience, as many others no doubt occurred during the intervening period.

It is interesting to note the conflicting emotions reported by the user group, particularly in response to this peak experience in adolescence. Stimulated but guilty as well, they want to copy the activity portrayed, but often wait months or years before accomplishing it. Here is a portion of an interview with a user that examines his key experience and its aftereffects.

INT.: *Of all these photographs, films, and books that you have mentioned seeing during your teens, which really stands out the most?*

RESP.: A photo of a girl with her dress up showing thighs, vulva, no panties.

INT.: *What about this photo makes it stand out in your mind so strongly?*

RESP.: The girl was pretty, smiling, enjoyed what she was doing. She was partially dressed which made the picture more erotic. Made me feel I was sneaking a look.

INT.: *Where did you see it?*

RESP.: Along the roadside.

INT.: *What about it was sexually exciting?*

RESP.: The girl's personal warmth. Her smile was exciting.

INT.: People often have more than one reaction, both pleasant and unpleasant. *What were your other feelings?*

RESP.: I had no bad feelings. I almost fell in love with the photo.

INT.: *Was there anything about sex in the photo that you had never heard of before?*

RESP.: First time I had a good close look at a woman's organs.

INT.: *What kind of sexual activity did you feel like engaging in after seeing the photo?*

RESP.: Straight intercourse. But I wasn't close to any girl then. Probably would have been too inhibited to try it.

INT.: *Of all these pictures, films, and books that you have seen during your teens, which one did you find the most sexually exciting?*

RESP.: *Lady Chatterly's Lover.*

INT.: *Could you tell me why?*

RESP.: It had the most complete accurate descriptions of intercourse and genitals; better done, more inspiring than "crude" stuff; I liked the the scene of screwing in the rain. I liked descriptions of feelings accompanying sex.

INT.: *Which one did you find the most disgusting?*

RESP.: A sadomasochistic picture I saw when I was eight years old.

INT.: *During your teens, in addition to these photographs, films, and books, what other things did usually turn you on? (You know, like clothing or objects of the same or opposite sex.)*

RESP.: Panties. Silk stockings with seams. Damp smell of woods.

A similar pattern may be seen in this excerpt from an interview with a homosexual.

INT.: *Of all these photographs, films, and books you have mentioned seeing during your teens, which really stands out in your mind the most?*

RESP.: A stack of porno pictures my friend had.

INT.:   *What about them made these pictures stand out in your mind so strongly?*

RESP.:   They excited me so much.

INT.:   *Could you tell me what was shown or described?*

RESP.:   They showed all the possible heterosexual things: vaginal, anal, and oral contacts.

INT.:   *What about it was sexually exciting?*

RESP.:   The depiction of the sex act; I concentrated on the male in each one. [Note: Even though the erotica portrayed heterosexual relations, this homosexual utilized it to satisfy his sexual interest by focusing exclusively upon the male figure in the erotica.]

INT.:   *Did you have any negative reactions to these pictures?*

RESP.:   Yes. I found it frustrating because the photos excited me but there was no immediate outlet for me to relieve myself.

INT.:   *Did anything about it disgust you?*

RESP.:   No.

INT.:   *Was there anything you found out about sex from the photos that later in life you learned was not so?*

RESP.:   I think some of the poses were unrealistic.

INT.:   *Was there anything shown or described in the photos that you wished you could later try? (i.e., new techniques, new ways of having sex?)*

RESP.:   Yes, everything; I tried it and liked it.

INT.:   *What kind of sexual activity did you feel like engaging in after seeing the photos?*

RESP.:   Oral copulation with a man.

INT.:   *Did you do it?*

RESP.:   No, not at that time. I mostly thought about it and masturbated.

The transsexual group displayed a lower frequency of negative emotions accompanying exposure, little desire to imitate the behavior expressed in the erotic stimulus, and, in fact, little actual imitation in later life. The following interviews with two different transsexuals illustrate these findings.

INT.	RESP. 1	RESP. 2
Of all these photographs, films, and books that you have mentioned seeing during your teens, which really stands out in your mind the most?	Pictures of men's and women's genitals.	Tijuana bibles.

INT.	RESP. 1	RESP. 2
What about it makes it stand out in your mind so strongly?	I thought they shouldn't have been taken; I thought it was nasty.	They were a little dirtier, more descriptive and picturesque.
What was shown or described?	———	Everything. All the sex acts.
What about it was sexually exciting?	I didn't find them exciting.	The sex act itself.
People often have more than one reaction, both pleasant and unpleasant. What were your other feelings?	I possibly had guilt feelings.	I wanted to be him, the man in the picture.
Did anything about it disgust you?	Yes. It degraded people.	The fact that the picture was taken.
Was there anything about sex that you had never heard of before?	No.	Sex with animals: I was seeing most of it for the first time.
What about sex did you learn from it?	Nothing.	New positions and things I'd never seen.
Was there anything shown or described that you wished you could later try?	I wished I was the man.	New ways of doing the same old thing: I wanted to try anal sex.
What kind of sexual activity did you feel like engaging in after seeing it?	If any, probably with another woman.	Anal sex with a man.
During your teens, in addition to these photos, films, and books, what other things turned you on?	Nothing.	Nothing.

Acquisition of erotica. Respondents were asked whether they obtained for themselves during adolescence erotic material of the type described in their most vivid experience. Generally, there were few group differences on this question. When respondents were asked how often they read or looked at this erotic material (if they had their own), some group differences emerged. Responses were divided into two categories, "a few times" or "regularly," and while 38 percent of the controls claimed regular usage of erotica similar to that described in their peak experience, 75 percent of the homosexuals ($p < .10$ vs. controls), 75 percent of the transsexuals ($p < .20$ vs. controls), and 90 percent of the users ($p < .05$ vs. controls) so reported. Thus, those members of the test samples reported looking at their own erotica more frequently than did the controls.

Note that these figures are based upon a minority of subjects in each group who actually obtained their own erotica. For example, 25 percent of controls, 40 percent of homosexuals, 25 percent of transsexuals, and 53 percent of the users reported obtaining their own erotica. Only the frequency of users differs significantly from controls ($p < .01$). Thus, a higher percentage of those in each group who obtained their own erotica report more frequent usage of the erotica than do controls. It is also worth noting that the future heavy consumer of pornography is likely to begin this practice in late adolescence.

These data should not be confused with the finding in chapter 5 that suggested that each of the test samples had less overall exposure to pornography than controls. This is still true. The data in the passage above merely indicate that the homosexuals and users were more likely to obtain some type of erotica of the sort they identify as most vivid during adolescence. As noted, this would usually be some sort of photo, and if they obtained one, they were more likely to refer to it than were the controls. Part of the apparent discrepancy is due to the fact that the test groups selected the stimuli from the early adolescent period as most exciting, and thus had many future opportunities to repeat the experience. The controls selected a more explicit stimulus (pornographic film) experienced in late adolescence that was less readily repeatable or obtainable. These findings, then, do not contradict the data reported in chapter 5 concerning the degree of exposure to erotica during adolescence.

After being asked whether they wished to imitate the activity shown in the most vivid erotic experience, respondents were asked to describe the type of sexual activity, if any, they felt like engaging in. These data were unexpected, to some degree. The homosexuals who did not evidence great interest in imitating the activities shown reported a desire for some type of nonheterosexual activity (44%, most citing masturbation; only 11% desired heterosexual activity [$p < .001$ vs. controls]). Typical responses included: "oral copulation with men" or "I identified with the woman" or "at the time, masturbation." Curiously enough, while the activities depicted were largely heterosexual, the desire stimulated in the homosexuals was one of a homosexual nature. This suggests that sexual arousal and sexual activity desired reflect different psychological processes.

In the transsexual sample, the predominant sexual activity desired after the peak experience was coded in the *other* category. This turned out to be answers like "sex as a woman" or "anal sex," when the actual data were scrutinized. Only 28 percent of the transsexuals desired heterosexual relations, and 14 percent homosexual relations. This pattern was also significantly different (p < .003) from the controls, in which 86 percent of the sample reported desiring heterosexual relations. The deep confusion felt by the transsexual concerning his sexual identity is reflected in his lack of desire for either heterosexual or homosexual activity.

The user sample was most akin to the controls (56% desiring heterosexual relations and 44% coded as *other,* almost exclusively masturbation). When the percentage of the sample who did desire some sexual activity was queried as to whether they actually engaged in that activity, marked group differences emerge. Of the twenty-nine controls who desired heterosexual relations, only 30 percent actually made any attempt to engage in them subsequent to the peak experience. Of the eighteen homosexuals who expressed a desire for some sexual activity, 59 percent carried through with it, and of these, half reported satisfaction with the experience and half did not. In the transsexual sample, of seven respondents who reported a desire for sexual activity, three had the experience; in the user sample, of thirty-six desiring some sexual activity, 70 percent performed the activity, and reported finding it largely satisfactory. By and large, in the latter sample the sexual activity engaged in was masturbation.

Frequency of exposure to vivid erotica. The respondents were asked to estimate the frequency of exposure to erotica like that described in the peak experience during their teen-age years. No significant group differences were found — the modal answer was "a few times." Note the difference here between these groups and the rapists, who did mention a reasonably high degree of exposure to their peak erotic stimulus.

When asked whether they had obtained any erotica like that in the peak experience as an adolescent, only one group differed from controls, the user sample in which 53 percent (p < .01 vs. 25% of controls) answered affirmatively. Thus, the adult pornography user had a tendency during his teen-age years to purchase erotica.

Frequency of thoughts about sex. There were no group differences registered in response to a question concerning how often the respondent thought about sex during his teen-age years, the modal answer being "a good part of the time." Note that this differs from the data presented for the sex offenders in the previous chapter.

When asked whether adolescent sexual fantasies incorporated some aspect of material portrayed in erotica encountered as a teen-ager, the modal answer was *yes*. For instance: "Well, usually it was a scene where I would be getting a piece, and how I would want it and get it." Other typical replies were: "I'd think of a big-busted woman sometimes" or "I'd remember scenes where a man is performing the sex act and I would think about intercourse and put myself in the situation." All groups differed from controls, of whom 67 percent answered affirmatively; only 37 percent of the transsexuals so answered ($p < .10$ vs. controls); and 84 percent of the users so answered ($p < .10$ vs. controls). Thus, transsexuals are less likely than controls to indicate that their adolescent sex fantasies were derived from erotica, and the users more likely to utilize segments of erotica in their fantasies.

Masturbation reactions. When the groups were asked how often they would think of aspects of an erotic stimulus during masturbation, the transsexuals and users stand out again. Sixty-one percent of the transsexual sample ($p < .004$) never associated masturbation with thoughts of erotic material, while the users sometimes did (53% weekly and 27% daily, $p < .01$): "Before I started having hetero activity I used to masturbate looking at pictures." "I remember flashing back to the scene in *Candy* where she has intercourse with the hunchback." The users also stood out from controls in their tendency to view erotica while masturbating as a teen-ager.

Most exciting stimulus. At the conclusion of this section of the interview, respondents were asked which type of erotic stimulus they saw as a teen-ager was most exciting. Control group answers were equally divided among printed matter (a book or magazine), photo, or a movie. This was also true of the user group. The homosexuals and transsexuals, however, differed in the low percentage reporting a movie (0% for transsexuals and 13% for homosexuals), and the high rate of those mentioning photos (60% for transsexuals and 70% for homosexuals). "To just take a book, for instance, I think most kids go through and look for the places which are particularly good. But a photograph is obvious and it's there. You're confronted with something which is still, so your imagination has to work around it to build up an idea of how this came about and what's going to transpire next. You make up a little story in your mind and this photograph is a part of it. This is a scene out of a movie which you're producing in your own mind." It is particularly interesting that photos of an erotic nature loom so large in the memories of sex offenders (see chap. 6) and nonheterosexual individuals. Of course, our data on frequency of exposure during adolescence suggest that all of these groups were less likely to have seen erotic films, and therefore were limited in what they could choose as their most exciting experience.

SUMMARY AND CONCLUSIONS

As in the previous chapter, it is helpful to consider by groups the patterns of reports concerning the most vivid experience with erotica during adolescence considered in this chapter.

Homosexuals. The respondents in this sample report a photo or book as most memorable; a photo manifestly heterosexual, but which in the "eye of the beholder" was frequently used to satisfy homosexual interests. This photo or book was typically encountered early in adolescence, as was the case for the groups covered in chapter 6. Arousal was the predominant emotion recalled, coupled with the sex guilt pattern of disgust. The educational function of this peak experience was particularly noteworthy for the homosexuals, as it was often their first exposure to full female nudity. If the experience depicted involved homosexual relations, it was also likely to stand out as the viewer's first encounter with that form of sexuality.

This most vivid experience was likely to linger in the imagination of the future homosexual, who usually wanted to imitate the activity represented. Actual imitation was rare, as initial homosexual experiences typically occurred years after this vivid contact with erotica. In some instance, the sexual behavior selected for imitation was based on homosexual erotica; however, in the great majority of reports, the peak erotic stimulus was designed to represent heterosexual relations. Yet the emerging homosexual selected for later recall those aspects of the stimulus commensurate with his emerging homosexual orientation. Females in heterosexual photos or books were selected as objects of identification for these males, and the role of the female in the sex act was erotically exciting to men. Or, conversely, they focused upon the male in the stimulus, not as an object of identification, but as an erotic object stimulating their fantasies. It is clear that a sharp distinction must be drawn between the intent of the creator of erotica and the use to which it is put by the recipient. A substantial number of homosexuals reported a desire to attempt some type of homosexual relations, despite the fact that the erotica depicted heterosexual relations.

In adolescence, the future homosexuals continued to be interested in erotica and look at it regularly, and most acquired some of their own. This activity was commensurate with their tendency to think about sex "a good part of the time" and to masturbate, utilizing thoughts based on previously experienced erotica.

The homosexuals report that during their adolescent years photos or books continued to be the most exciting medium of erotic representation for them. They frequently mention aesthetic criteria for judging erotica, a concern that was particularly characteristic of this sample. The quality of photography or writing often influenced the impact of an erotic stimulus for them, a consideration more likely to appear in the interviews of female respondents in our experience.

Transsexuals. This group, superficially paralleling the homosexual sample in that both groups manifested clear-cut sex-role inversion, actually appears very different in its reports of response to erotica as teen-agers. They do identify a photo experienced in early adolescence as most vivid, but they are less likely to report the ambivalent responses of arousal and disgust to this stimulus than do homosexuals, resembling controls in this reaction. They do, however, share the homosexuals' tendency to find this vivid piece of erotica educational, but their concern is with the depiction of heterosexual relations as opposed to the homosexuals' more basic curiosity about nudity.

The transsexuals differ from the homosexuals in that few, if any, expressed the retrospective desire to imitate activities represented in this vivid erotic stimulus. The sexual activity transsexuals desired following this peak adolescent experience related more often to their desires for sexual transformation than to any activity represented in erotica. Once again we see the lack of consistency between sexual response and the activity represented in an erotic stimulus. Similarly, the transsexuals report little masturbation tied to themes derived from erotica, preferring their own self-generated fantasies as stimuli.

Users. This group does not differ from controls in the type of erotic stimulus identified as most vivid, but, like the nonheterosexual groups, specifies an experience from an earlier age period than the controls. They report a combination of guilt and arousal as their reaction to the erotica, unlike the homosexuals who are more likely to mention disgust as part of their ambivalent pattern. Novelty was an important aspect of this vivid memory, as the users indicated it was often their first introduction to the mechanics of heterosexual relations. Respondents in the user sample were most likely to report that some aspect of the erotica would linger in their imaginations and that they wanted to imitate some specific type of sexual behavior portrayed — typically, heterosexual intercourse. They were, in fact, likely to translate this desire into behavior, but at a much later age, and to report satisfaction with the experience. The user reports a high degree of interest in erotica during his teen-age years, regularly looking at material similar to that described in his most vivid experience and, in fact, obtaining some of his own. So, the user's tendency to acquire erotica usually begins during adolescence. The user reports being generally preoccupied with thoughts of sex during his teen-age years, and is most likely of all groups to incorporate segments of erotica into his masturbatory activity. This habit, as other data indicate, carries through to the user's adult life as well.

Reading about sex will get anybody excited.

*It [an erotic book] was interesting to read but
I didn't get aroused over it.*

TWO FEMALE OBJECT PEDOPHILES

8

PEAK ADULT EXPERIENCE
WITH EROTICA: SEX OFFENDERS

In the previous chapters we have examined the impact of erotic stimuli experienced during the formative years of preadolescence and adolescence upon attitudes and behavior, especially in later life. Our purpose was to establish whether the early experiences of any group studied (sex offenders, nonheterosexuals, users, and controls) were significantly different from those of the other three groups, and whether any correlation existed between these experiences and subsequent sexual maladjustment. In this chapter and those that follow, our concern shifts to the role and function of erotica in the adult lives of our respondents — the degree to which they encounter erotica, its impact on their attitudes, and its role, if any, in their sexual lives. In particular, we shall focus on the degree to which erotic stimuli relate to the behavior of the sex offenders and nonheterosexuals in our samples.

We begin by analyzing the data on sex offenders, and proceed in chapter 9 to the homosexual, transsexual, and user groups. In chapter 10, we turn to the general topic of sexual fantasy and its relationship to erotica.

The data in chapters 8 and 9 are based upon responses covering the year prior to the interview. Since most of the sex offenders were at that time inmates of Atascadero State Hospital, the focus of their interview was on the year immediately prior to institutionalization.

Type of stimulus selected as most vivid. Respondents were asked to specify the nature of the stimulus in their most vivid contact with erotica during the specified year. Being older, and therefore having greater access to erotica, all groups typically cited more explicit materials than were mentioned for the adolescent years; and specific stimuli (photos, books, films, live shows) were not confined to certain groups (as had been the case with data for adolescence).

Here are some examples of the types of erotica specified as most vivid in adulthood:

RESP. 1: A live topless show stands out the most. It stands out in my memory because it was live, it was right there in front of you. It showed everything from the waist up. I saw it in a bar in San Francisco.

RESP. 2: Nudes in *Playboy* stand out the most. They were all voluptuous-type women, very attractive girls with perfect smooth bodies. One in particular stands out because she was facing away from the camera, but looking back over her shoulder and her buttocks were visible. It was particularly exciting because the girl had a bikini bottom on and a see-through cape and some costume jewelry.

RESP. 3: I guess I'd have to say the book *Candy* stands out most in my mind. It was the fact that she was so naïve and seducible, like in the one scene when she met a man that was supposed to be psychic and he induced her to have intercourse with him through conning and trickery.

It was probably inevitable at least one respondent would select a book on sadomasochism.

RESP. 4 (a rapist): The book *Marquis de Sade* stands out most in my recent memory — the brutality made it stand out so clearly. One scene in particular stands out when a guy had this girl hanging with a noose around her neck and screwing her at the same time; then when he finished, he kicked the basket out from under her. I learned that I got turned on by brutality.

Social context of exposure. When asked who they were with at the time of this most vivid experience, two of the three sex offender groups gave answers that differed sharply from those of the control group. Table 15 indicates that both the rapists and the male object pedophiles were less likely to experience their peak erotic stimulus in a social context, involving friends of the same or opposite sex.

Table 15

OTHERS PRESENT DURING RECENT PEAK EXPERIENCE

Subjects	Alone (%)	With Friend of Same Sex (%)	With Friend of Opposite Sex (%)	p
Rapists	58	32	10	.002
Male object pedophiles	63	26	10	.001
Female object pedophiles	22	39	39	
Controls	16	42	42	

Emotions aroused by erotica. Respondents in all groups were likely to experience sexual arousal from this peak erotic stimulus, and there were no significant group differences in the frequency of these reports. As in the adolescent reports, however, all three groups of sex offenders reported a higher frequency of associated negative emotions (shame, guilt, disgust, etc.) than the controls. The differences were statistically significant only when the rapists were compared to controls (p < .05). Here are some representative samples of these negative emotional reactions from the rapists: "When I saw it [a man performing cunnilingus in a live show in Mexico], I felt it was sickening." "In the book, one story dealing with homosexuality disgusted me." In response to a topless dancer, "It upset me to think that she made her money that way — I mean, she was a pretty girl and I dug her — it was upsetting." The rapist who found the *Marquis de Sade* particularly vivid also said, "I felt pretty guilty; no matter how wicked you are, you *know* these things are wrong!"

Interesting group differences emerged when we asked whose idea it was to look at this erotic stimulus. Half of the controls indicated it was their idea and half attributed the idea to friends. Among the rapists and female object pedophiles, those who claimed to be with others at the time of the peak erotic experiences attributed the motivation for exposure to their friends.

Respondents were also asked whether they wished to imitate the specific sexual activities represented in the erotica selected as most vivid. In the adolescent reports, a large proportion of the respondents (see chapter 7) did indicate such a desire. When the focus was on adulthood, however, only 38 percent of the rapists, 38 percent of the male object pedophiles, 26 percent of the female object pedophiles, and 32 percent of the controls wished to copy in an exact manner some aspect of behavior represented in the erotica.

While specific imitation was rare (sometimes for the simple reason

that the unusual circumstances could not be duplicated), the respondent usually channeled his aroused sexual energy into some more available outlet. One subject described a game he frequently played at the
local magazine stand. "I'd go into the bookstores and look on the magazine racks and thumb through 'em and look at pictures of nudes. I get
kinda turned on by that. In fact, I had a little game I would play sometimes. I would wait until a woman was standing there and I'd sometimes kneel down and start opening 'em to the nudes so she could see me
lookin' at 'em. And I was kinda gettin' turned on by doing this, hoping
that sayin' 'Ha, Ha, look at this' to her would maybe embarrass her or
something. Just kind of a little game I was playing. And I'd do this if it
was an older lady or if it was a young girl. Kind of a fun game. And this
was prior to the rapes I started doing this."

Sexual arousal was acknowledged by the majority, but not all,
respondents in the four groups. ("The film didn't stimulate me to have
sexual activity." "No, nothing desired.") Of those respondents who did
desire sexual activity, the activity mentioned was more likely to parallel
current sexual patterns than the experience represented in the erotica.
Desires stimulated by erotica included the following: "Intercourse."
"Feeling the girl's breasts [referring to girls in topless show]." "Sexual
intercourse." "Just going to bed with a girl." "I would've like to make it
with somebody." And the respondent who previously suggested the
Marquis de Sade as his favorite erotica reported, "I did think I would
like to rape and torture women." A pedophile, male object, reported
a desire to molest a child after reading a piece of erotica describing
child molestation.

Others alleviated their sexual urge by masturbation ("I wanted to
have intercourse," said one rapist, "but I ended up masturbating") or
relations with a wife, girlfriend, or another man. For the rapist, particularly, masturbation was often preferable to risking a problematical and
possibly violent session with a woman. "A lot of times I had a woman
available at the time and I would take the pictures and end up masturbating to the pictures instead of going into the other room and having
sex with the woman."

Of the small number of respondents desiring to act out some aspect
of the sexual behavior portrayed in this peak erotic stimulus, three
rapists indicated that they actually did so, as did three male object pedophiles, five female object pedophiles, and six controls. Typically, the
imitation occurred some time after a stimulus had been experienced.
Immediate precipitation of sexual activity by erotica was rarely if ever
mentioned. More often, when subsequent sexual activity was discussed,
the relationship between exposure to erotica and the actual sexual activity
was more complex. For example, the following episode described by a

female object pedophile respondent who committed incest contains memories not only of erotica, but also of arousal triggered by the subject's relationship with his daughter. "I had heard but did not know for sure that teen-age girls were hot for sex, but I learned this in the book [*Teenage Erotica*] and from observing my own daughter. I learned that young girls were very interested in sex. . . . I believe that was what influenced me to have sexual intercourse with my daughter."

When the small number of respondents who did imitate the erotica were asked about their emotional reaction to their attempt, the sex offenders reported dissatisfaction while the controls were generally more satisfied.

Incorporation of material from peak experiences with sex fantasies. Since most respondents did not attempt imitation of sexual activities portrayed in erotica, we asked what aspects of the observed sexual experience were likely to become part of the individual's sex fantasies or daydreams.

First we inquired how often, as a rule, the subjects daydreamed about sex. As with the adolescent data, the rapists stand out from all other groups: 67 percent said "always" (p < .004 vs. controls). "Most of the time I was out on bail for rape . . . I was always thinking about sex whether I wanted to or not." Only 11 percent male object pedophiles, 26 percent female object pedophiles, and 22 percent controls were included in the "always" category. Thus, the tendency of the rapists toward constant preoccupation with sex is consistent through adolescence and maturity.

Generally, only a small percentage of the controls (9%) mentioned that themes from their most vivid adult experiences with erotica turned up in their sex fantasies or daydreams. "I visualize the person I've had the best sexual experience with. A live person is more interesting than a book!" This absence of identifiable themes contrasts markedly with their adolescent linking of stimulus and fantasy. The rapists and the male object pedophiles however, do indicate that aspects of erotica are present in their daydreams. For example, 55 percent of the rapists said that scenes depicting heterosexual intercourse were transferred from the erotic source (photo, book, film, etc.) to their fantasy life (p < .001 vs. controls) and 30 percent of the male object pedophiles agreed (p < .065 vs. controls). For depictions of oral sex, 20 percent of the male object pedophiles (p < .04 vs. 2% controls) indicated some reappearance in their subsequent daydreams.

While most people would not consider *The Boston Strangler* an erotic film likely to reappear in one's sexual fantasies, several of the rapists found the strangler's ability to dominate and physically subdue his women victims to be a source of sexual imagery. "It was mostly not violence, beating them up or killing them, it was mostly having it the way you like it, ripping their clothes off and throwing them on the bed." Despite the murders, "I got an exciting feeling, sex rushed through me watching him do that." Some of the rapists fantasized about rapes they had previously committed in which their performance contrasted woefully with their actual desires. "Hiding and waiting for the girl to walk along at night and doing a lot of things I was too scared to do when I actually did it." "I'd fantasize why didn't I stay there fifteen or twenty more minutes and have more complete intercourse . . . caress her, oral-copulate her . . . her oral-copulate me . . . having her reach her climax."

Motorcycle films containing violence and "gang bangs" frequently nourished erotic fantasy. As one rapist put it, "I'd think of some of the girls I had raped. [And] some of the girls that got raped in the movies. Place myself in the villain's place instead of the hero's. You know, I had a rough, a hardened image."

It is less common to find such well-defined fantasy formations in the responses of the pedophile groups. While they can picture in their minds fondling young boys or girls, the eventual experience is often a mundane occurrence, just part of their everyday routine. "Living in a trailer court them kids would come around and want to suck your dick or jack you off for two bits right there." Most respondents indicated that their adult sex fantasies were not likely to involve fictional characters. As one pedophile, male object, put it, "My daydreams are about *real* people."

The respondents were subsequently asked what emotions they felt when scenes from erotica reappeared in their daydreams. Positive emotions were arousal and curiosity; negative emotions were shame, disgust, repulsion. Of the controls, 86 percent reported positive emotions when scenes of erotica reappeared in their daydreams. A similar pattern was found for the two pedophile groups (77% of male object pedophiles and 100% of female object pedophiles). The rapists, however, stand out here, as 58 percent reported positive emotions and 41 percent negative reactions: the same combination of arousal and disgust rapists reported as their adolescent reaction to erotica reappears in their adult reports. "Yeah, when I think about those books, something makes me kind of angry about all women. They kind of have this angle — they have something that you need and they kind of tempt you with it and flaunt themselves. Make the man be the chaser." Or as another rapist reported, "The whole thing of it disgusted me because I was so attracted to it."

Relationships to masturbation. Respondents were asked how often erotic material of the type portrayed in their most vivid experience excited them to masturbate or attempt sexual relations. The data for this question, as well as others dealing with masturbation are presented in table 16. These data indicate that rapists and male object pedophiles frequently masturbate while thinking of previously experienced erotica. This is not true for the female object pedophiles or the controls.

Both rapists and male object pedophiles report a generally high rate of masturbation, and in the latter group the rate of regular masturbation is higher *without* erotica than with (44% vs. 16%). The data for the controls indicate a marked difference from adolescent patterns, where a high rate of masturbation stimulated by recall of erotica was reported (see chap. 6). In the sex offender samples, however, there is little change from the adolescent pattern of masturbating in response to erotica.

When asked how often thoughts of erotica led them to attempt sexual relations (either homosexual or heterosexual) with another person (see bottom of table 16), a marked contrast can be seen in the rapist sam-

Table 16

RESPONSES TO EROTICA BY SEX OFFENDERS AND CONTROLS

Stimuli and Subjects	Never (%)	Occasionally (%)	Regularly (%)	p
Thoughts of erotic material excites to masturbation				
Rapists	20	55	25	.001
Pedo M	33	49	16	.02
Pedo F	47	46	6	—
Controls	60	40	0	—
Masturbation when not thinking of erotic material				
Rapists	21	53	26	.06
Pedo M	22	33	44	.02
Pedo F	37	26	37	.13
Controls	54	32	13	—
Thoughts of erotica excite to sexual relations				
Rapists	42	36	21	—
Pedo M	29	53	17	—
Pedo F	39	33	28	.11
Controls	44	49	7	—

ple: 42 percent indicate "never." Thus, while masturbation is a common response to erotica in the rapist group, attempts at sexual relations are much rarer. "I wanted to have sex with a girl, but I could never really picture myself doing it — always afraid of being put down." It was worth noting that all three sex offender groups, taken as a whole, did indicate a higher percentage of respondents answering "regularly" than do controls.

The controls most often answered that the main stimulus to sexual relations was some activity by their regular sex partner or thoughts of that partner. "Having intercourse with my wife — that's what I fantasy about." "Just having a woman that I've worked with at the office and feel attracted to." "Just a girl I knew back East — I'd think of her and really get turned on by fantasies. They're more real than any book or picture." Such fantasies became their most significant erotica during their adult years. It is interesting to note the marked developmental shift shown by the controls, in contrast with the sex offenders, toward attaching greater erotic value to *real* than to *symbolic* representations of erotica.

General experience with erotica during recent period. Respondents were also asked which item out of the total erotica to which they had been exposed during the year in question was most sexually exciting to them. Few differences among the sex offenders and controls were found in the answers to this question. Only the male object pedophiles stand out in reporting that they found homosexual erotica most exciting ($p < .01$ vs. controls).

When the groups were asked which medium of expression was most exciting (photos, written descriptions, movies, live shows), marked intergroup differences appeared. Almost half of the rapists (47%) reported that they found a written description of sex most exciting while only 15 percent of the controls so reported ($p < .07$ rapists vs. controls). Of the controls 38 percent reported a live sex show, and 28 percent a movie, as most sexually exciting. Thus, the controls are consistent from adolescence to adulthood in reporting the most explicit representation of sexuality as most erotic, while the rapists tend to select less direct forms of erotica (photos as adolescents, written material as adults) as most erotic. Neither of the other two groups of institutionalized sex offenders differed significantly from the controls in the preferred medium of erotica, except that male object pedophiles were less likely ($p < .05$) to report a live show than controls (16% vs. 38%, respectively).

The respondents were also asked to identify the erotic stimuli seen recently that had most disgusted or repulsed them. Their negative reactions were prompted by a variety of sexual aberrations such as incest ("fantasies about my daughter were pleasant and disgusting at the same time"), sex with animals ("the woman with the dog was most disgusting), or homosexuality. The rapist sample emerged as the group most likely to find sadomasochistic material "most disgusting" (25% vs. 6% controls, p < .08). One rapist subject out on bail, who constantly found himself watching motorcycle movies, was simultaneously turned on and off by the violence and "gang bangs" that were an inevitable component of his choice. It is sometimes impossible to separate the subject's specific sexual dislikes from a general (if unconscious and thus undefined) antipathy to sexual experience.

Current contact with erotica similar to that selected as most vivid. Respondents were also asked how often they had seen erotica of the type that "turned them on" during the previous year. (The sex offenders in general had reported less exposure to erotica than other groups during the year in question.) No significant group differences emerged from this data. For example, reports of "many" exposures were found for 25 percent of the rapists, 17 percent of the male object pedophiles, 28 percent of the female object pedophiles, and 25 percent of the controls.

There was a slight variation among the percentages of those in each sex offender group who wished to obtain their own erotica, but the difference was not statistically significant. When the sex offender groups are taken as a single sample (averaging 46% rapists, 59% male object pedophiles, and 50% female object pedophiles) and contrasted with the 29 percent of controls who expressed a desire to obtain their own erotica, the difference is significant (p < .05).

Of those sex offenders who expressed a desire to obtain their own erotica, a high percentage did, in fact, obtain their own. Over half of the controls who wished to have their own erotica did not have any, while 100 percent of the rapists, 80 percent of the male object pedophiles, and 83 percent of the female object pedophiles who expressed a desire to have their own erotica did in fact obtain some. Further, those institutionalized sex offenders who did obtain their own erotica reported looking at it more often than did the controls (p < .05 for all sex offenders vs. controls).

To summarize the foregoing: (1) equal percentages of institutionalized sex offenders and controls desired their own erotica; (2) a higher percentage of institutionalized sex offenders who desired erotica obtained it than a comparable sample of controls; (3) of those who actually obtained erotica in all samples, a higher percentage of sex offenders than controls looked at it frequently. In all, however, only a small minority of sex offenders obtain their own erotica and who use it regularly.

Impact of erotica experienced recently. Unlike the adolescent reports, these data showed that few respondents in any group learned anything about sex from erotica encountered as an adult. If erotica seen recently was recalled as novel, it was usually because the individual had not previously been exposed to representations of homosexuality, group sex, or explicit nudity as in a live show. In the case of sex offenders, it is crucial to consider whether exposure to erotica preceded the commission of a criminal act. Generally, the sex offenders denied that exposure to erotica was a significant variable in the commission of their sex crimes and, in fact, often specified what they felt were more significant stimuli. This attitude, common to all three groups of sex offenders, is represented in the two segments of interviews below, the first with a rapist and the second with a female object pedophile.

INTERVIEW WITH RAPIST

INT.: *Did you come across the idea of rape in any of the erotic materials that you have seen?*

RESP.: No.

INT.: *How old were you when you first started having the fantasies?*

RESP.: I can't say when the desire to have sex with a woman and fantasies about rape would separate. About the first thing that I can recall about rape must have been three years ago. I read in a magazine where it recounted — I don't know if it was *McCall's* or *Ladies' Home Journal* — about a woman that a man used a knife to make her be quiet and raped her. And then he escaped or something. All this, while her little daughter had to look on. I remember reading that when I was twenty-five years old. But I can't say that the fantasy of rape started with this article, but it does stick out in my mind. I think the fantasy of rape probably started occurring regularly six years or so before I started raping. I'd get sexually excited by gals down at the beach or something and I'd want to have sex with them. But, I wouldn't know how to approach them or meet them. So, I'd follow them home and rape them.

INTERVIEW WITH FEMALE OBJECT PEDOPHILE

INT.: *Did anything that you read or saw stimulate you to fantasy about young girls or think of approaching them sexually?*

RESP.: I don't know what you mean, those things don't do much to me. Like I say, it has to be the real thing as I can't fantasy — fantasy is not in my line of thinking.

INT.: *Well, did you ever see or read anything about child molesting that gave you the idea to do this or excited you in this way?*

RESP.: No, usually when I approached a child I was half-drunk.

INT.:   *What happens to you when you get drunk?*
RESP.: I'd want sex when I was drinking. But, I never could communicate
with adult women, so in the past I'd go to a prostitute rather than
go home to my wife. Once I was half-drunk and thinking about sex
and I came across these little girls, four different times actually, and I
molested them. I didn't have intercourse with them, I didn't hurt
them in any way. I don't know what it is, it [the child molesting] hurt
me. I'm going to AA now, I don't want to take any more chances
with booze.

SUMMARY AND CONCLUSIONS

If we compare the findings cited above with those of chapter 6
which focus upon adolescent experience with erotica, a number of clear
differences emerge. First, adults are less likely to find their contacts with
erotica educational than they did as adolescents. If these contacts do
serve an educational function, it is to introduce the person to more
exotic types of sexual relations. The most prominent reaction to erotica
as adults is sexual arousal, experienced pleasurably by the controls and
more ambivalently by the sex offenders. There is no clear-cut pattern
of sexual activity following this arousal, and performance of specific
antisocial sexual acts suggested or elicited by this heightened state of
arousal is rarely reported by the sex offenders. The pattern of sexual
behavior manifested appears to be a response to a highly complex set
of stimuli of which erotica is but one factor. Lowered inhibitions via
alcohol, rejection of wives or lovers ("I came home one night and
wanted to have sexual relations with my wife. She hadn't let me make
love to her for months and she wasn't any different that night. I lay
there frustrated, furious and wild with desire. I finally got disgusted and
went downtown and raped this woman who I followed home. All through
the rape, I fantasied that I was making love to my wife"), or associa-
tions with peer groups advocating deviant sexual patterns ("I was going with this group who were all into the sadomasochism thing. I was
tremendously turned on by the whole idea and couldn't think of anything
but rape for weeks until finally I seemed to go out of control and did
rape somebody myself") seemed highly significant in releasing antisocial
sexual behavior.

Still we cannot deny completely the role of erotica in stimulating
thoughts and desires of sexual relations. It does seem that the intentions
of the creator of the erotic stimulus do not always parallel the reaction
produced. For example, *The Boston Strangler* hardly qualifies as erotica,
yet the violence was stimulating to the rapist quoted above. The genre
of motorcycle gang movies, so common a few years ago, is more di-

rectly sexual in intent, and once again a rapist in our sample found the violence stimulating. But, what of the description of a rape by a house-wife in the *Ladies' Home Journal*? Would anyone suggest that this was meant to constitute an erotic stimulus likely to activate desires of rape? Hardly, so we must consider that (sex offenders are highly receptive to suggestions of sexual behavior congruent with their previously formed desires and will interpret the material at hand to fit their needs.) It is true, however, that while few, if any, sex offenders suggest that erotica played a role in the commission of sex crimes, stimuli expressing bru-tality, with or without concomitant sexual behavior, were often men-tioned as disturbing, by rapists in particular. This raises the question of whether the stimulus most likely to release antisocial sexual behavior is one representing sexuality, or one representing aggression.

The contrast between the sex offenders and controls in the type of sexual activity associated with erotica is significant. While all groups used masturbation as an outlet during teen-age years, the control sample generally did not continue as adults; sex offenders, however, kept up the practice. Fantasy objects decline in arousal value for the normally developing male, and *real* people become the source of his sex fantasies. The sex offenders are more like teen-agers in their sexual orientations, still highly stimulated by fantasy objects and fixated upon masturbation as a sexual outlet. This appears to be but one aspect of a generally lower level of social competence and adequacy when contrasted with the con-trols (see chap. 4).

*A man is playing with this girl
after they've had intercourse, then they have anal intercourse;
it stands out because I'd like to try it.*

A HOMOSEXUAL

9

PEAK ADULT EXPERIENCE
WITH EROTICA: HOMOSEXUALS,
TRANSSEXUALS, USERS

Chapter 8 presented data on experience with erotica during the year prior to the interview for the sex offenders. We turn now to the homosexual, transsexual, and user samples. As with the sex offender groups, there were few if any differences between the controls and these three samples concerning the type of erotic stimulus identified as most vivid during the previous year. Homosexuals and users had a higher proportion of respondents (36% and 34%, respectively, $p < .10$ for both groups vs. controls) who identified a pornographic film as most vivid; only 7 percent of the transsexuals identified that type of erotic stimulus as significant for them.

A series of questions in our interview dealt with aspects of the "peak" erotic stimulus that made it special for the respondent. There were no differences in the responses to these questions by the institutionalized sex offenders and controls. The homosexuals (58%), however, frequently identified an erotic stimulus as memorable because of its aesthetic quality ($p < .001$ vs. 22% of the controls who identified this quality). "The drawings were so beautifully done that they impressed me deeply," said one homosexual. Another said, "The people in the film were so handsome and the scenery was so attractive that it really turned me on." A third added: "I object to the male pictures that throw their crotch in your face. I think that the whole body is more appealing than merely the sex organs alone."

The users also mentioned aesthetic qualities in the stimulus more often than controls or transsexuals, but not at statistically significant levels. The users do stand out from all other groups (36% vs. 12% controls, p < .001) by virtue of identifying the explicitness of detail in the erotic stimulus as a significant contributor to their recent peak experience. "You could see all the sexual organs so clearly and the photography was so good that it really impressed me." "At certain moments, the camera focused on the participants' faces with such clarity that you felt that you were really 'right in' the sexual experience." For many respondents, the musical show *Hair* was a peak experience because it cast customary inhibitions aside, making "carefree references to heterosexual and homosexual love without the guilt and the shame and the hush-hush."

When asked to describe the type of sexual activity shown in this most vivid erotic stimulus, the controls and users most often mentioned some type of heterosexual activity:

User No. 1: The movie *I Am Curious Yellow,* stands out most in my mind. It was so daring — showing a completely nude male, a lot of intercourse and group sex.

User No. 2: A stag film stands out most where a woman was sucking this man and when he came he poured it out and squirted in her face. I don't know why — it just appealed to me and I enjoyed it.

Control No. 1: A little broad that I saw at a topless and bottomless place stands out most. I like small women and she had a perfect body. She had an art of taking her clothes off. She really belongs in a top-notch strip joint — she really had class. She was a good dancer and the way she took off her clothes was appealing.

Control No. 2: The movie *Midnight Cowboy* stands out. I recall it so strongly because they were able to use the erotic situations in good form and they go along with the theme of the movie, rather than being put in the film just to attract the public. The cruelty of sex was portrayed so vividly.

Only 19 percent of the homosexuals mentioned heterosexual activity as part of this most vivid experience, while 58 percent (vs. 8% controls, p < .0001) mentioned homosexual activity. ("Movies showing two men having sex." "The play *Geese,* it was so well done, particularly the scene when the two kids told their parents they were gay.") Almost one-third of the transsexuals (29%) also mentioned that homosexual activity was present in the vivid erotic stimulus seen recently. (*"Midnight Cowboy* is the thing that comes to mind. It really brought it home as it delved in the fringes of homosexuality and I could relate to it easily." "A book, *The Exhibition,* stands out — the way it was written — there wasn't anything left out. It was those girls' lives [in the book], it told exactly what they did — they were teasers. One girl had an affair with her girl cousin, for example.") The majority of the transsexuals' answers, however, were often more diffuse than those of the homosexuals. ("Pictures of girls with certain hair-dos stand out. I think hair is an indication of the character of a person." "Stag films stand out. They showed more than I thought possible; every picture had the girl's legs spread apart.")

Context of the peak experience. Respondents were asked whether this most vivid contact with an erotic stimulus occurred in their home or somewhere else. Nearly all indicated that it had occurred outside of their own homes. A substantial percentage of the users, nevertheless (48% vs. 25% controls, $p < .03$) viewed the erotica in their own home.

The suggestion that alcohol or other drugs may have played a part in this most vivid recent contact with erotica was vehemently denied by both homosexuals and transsexuals (85% and 100% answering negatively). Among the users and controls, however, 27 percent and 43 percent mentioned that alcohol was part of the peak experience; 22 percent and 16 percent identified other drugs. When drugs or alcohol were components of the experience, approximately half the respondents in each group believed that they had no effect on their reaction to the piece of erotica (59% users, 50% controls) while the balance of each sample felt that these agents heightened their enjoyment.

The presence or absence of companions during the peak experience varied from group to group. The controls were almost equally divided in reporting that they were with a friend of the opposite or same sex. A small number (16%) reported being alone, as opposed to 39 percent of transsexuals $p < .05$ vs. controls) and 33 percent of the users ($p < .05$ vs. controls). If the transsexuals were with someone else, it was typically a friend of the same sex, as was almost uniformly true for the homosexuals. As with controls, the balance of the users were equally divided between reports of being with friends of the same or opposite sex. Generally, respondents indicated that the reactions of the other person present either had no effect on them or enhanced their reaction.

Sexual desires stimulated by peak experience. Did the respondents identify any type of sexual activity portrayed in the most vivid erotic stimulus that they wished to try later? As with the sex offenders, the desire to imitate erotica drops very sharply as compared with reports focused on the adolescent period. Approximately one-third (32% and 36%, respectively) of the controls and homosexuals reported a desire to imitate this peak erotic stimulus. A significantly larger percentage (58%, p < .02 vs. controls) of the users reported a desire to imitate erotica, and a significantly lower percentage (17%, p < .05 vs. controls) of transsexuals expressed this type of desire.

Very few respondents stated that they actually carried through the desire into action. A close reading of these answers contributes a definite impression that the mature homosexual, user, or control has achieved some stable pattern in his sexual habits that he is unlikely to change. "Sure it might be nice once in a while, to have an orgy," is the gist of many replies, but we guess that most such wishes are purposefully unfulfilled. Anal intercourse may sound "vaguely interesting" and the occasional sexual perfectionist is still picking up "new ways to eat pussy" from stag films, but in general we sense a lack of enthusiasm about new techniques, which the statistics support. Of the ten homosexuals who wanted to copy the activity shown in the stimulus, only one actually carried it out. Of the twenty-seven users who mentioned imitation, half carried it out. Of the controls, six out of fourteen self-styled "imitators" mirrored the chosen sex activity. Thus, only in the user group do we find a large number of respondents who translated the desire to imitate erotica into active sexual behavior. In the homosexual and transsexual samples, such imitation was very rare. Generally, those respondents who did imitate some aspect of erotica found the experience satisfying — unlike the rapists, who were disappointed with their initial experiences.

Excerpts from some of the interviews covering the peak experience section of the questionnaire follow, starting with two homosexuals:

INT.	RESP. 1	RESP. 2
Of all these photographs, movies, books and live shows that you have seen within the past year, which really stands out in your mind the most?	A sadomasochistic film.	*Hair.*
What about it makes it stand out in your mind so strongly?	The one guy used his own masculine domination to make the	The people in the show were love-people. They're free, not up-

INT.	RESP. 1	RESP. 2
	other guy subservient; it was the domination that appealed to me, not that the other guy was in pain.	tight about sex. They don't make a big thing of it. They don't make it dirty.
Could you tell me what was shown or described? Which scene or episode particularly stands out in your mind?	The one guy was forcing the other guy to take his dick in his mouth.	The whole experience stands out.
Where did you see it?	In a person's private home.	Los Angeles, in a theater.
Were you using alcohol, pot, or other stuff at the time?	No.	Grass before and during. It made me more aware.
Was there anything in what you saw that you had not heard of before?	I had never seen anyone put a rubber band or clamp around the gonads to keep the blood in the penis and keep an erection.	No.
Was there anything shown or described that you wished you could later try?	Forcing someone to take your dick in his mouth. I wanted someone to fuck me in the mouth and I wanted to fuck somebody in the ass.	Not particularly. Just the normal thing. Seeking a partner and doing it.
What about your experience really turned you on?	The domination in the sadomasochism film.	The vibrancy and sexiness of the people.
Did anything disgust you?	No.	I was disgusted by some people in the audience. They left.

Here are the reactions of two users to the same section of the interview.

INT.	RESP. 1	RESP. 2
Of all these photographs, movies, books, and live shows that you have seen within the past year, which really stands out in your mind the most?	A book called *The Way of a Man With a Maid.*	*Fanny Hill.*
What about it stands out so strongly?	It made me very horny.	Some scenes were very stimulating.
Could you tell me what was shown or described?	A man is playing with this girl. After they've had regular intercourse, then they have anal sex.	Mutual masturbation. "#69." Homosexual mutual oral copulation.
Were you using alcohol or pot at the time?	Alcohol and/or pot before or during. It makes me more relaxed.	Sometimes grass but it's not a necessity.
Was there anything in what you read that you had not heard of before?	No.	No.
What about sex did you learn from this book?	I've never seen anybody have anal intercourse, but here it was described.	Particular new positions.
Was there anything shown or described that you wished you could later try?	Anal sex particularly, but after reading this book I just wanted some kind of sex. It really didn't matter as long as it was enjoyable.	Just ridding myself of inhibitions and doing things I've never done. Like I managed to get up and just take off my clothes, and I've recently gotten into homosexual activity and I've done just about everything possible.

While users are, obviously, not immune to guilt feelings about some of their sexual activities, they nevertheless are strongly motivated to free themselves from so-called sexual "hangups." This motivation energizes their search for new experiences and their ability to accept new roles in changing sexual contexts. Whether by will or skill, the user is determined to be sexually enlightened.

Finally, here are segments of interviews with two transsexuals.

INT.	RESP. 1	RESP. 2
Of all these photographs, movies, books, and live shows that you have seen within the past year, which really stands out the most?	*Midnight Cowboy.*	The hetero-sex in *Curious Yellow.*
What about it makes it stand out in your mind so strongly?	It dealt with the fringes of homosexuality. I could relate to it easily.	She was a pacifist and I identified with her almost completely.
Could you tell me what was shown or described?	The heterosexual act. It gave the impression of oral sex between the males. Then there was the psychological homosexual relation between the men.	Hetero activity. One oral-genital scene.
Were you using alcohol, pot or other stuff at the time?	No.	No.
Was there anything in what you saw that you had not heard of before?	No.	I had never seen a completely nude woman dancing before.
Was there anything new you learned about sex from this experience?	No.	No.
Was there anything shown or described that you wished you could later try?	Being a female.	No. I know my limitations.

INT.	RESP. 1	RESP. 2
What kind of sexual activity did you feel like engaging in afterwards?	I didn't.	Hetero-sex as a woman.
What about it was sexually exciting, and really turned you on?	Jon Voight.	Hetero activity.
Did anything disgust you?	It was a very sad movie.	No.

Though these transsexuals described different kinds of erotica as most exciting, both experienced a desire for sexual relations as a member of the opposite sex. This was quite typical of the transsexual's reaction to erotica. The dominant theme of their interviews is their desire to be a member of the opposite sex. While the erotica they describe might focus on normal heterosexual relations, it merely excites their transsexual desires.

Incorporation of erotica into one's sexual life. First, respondents were asked to estimate how often they daydreamed about sex. Though significant group differences appeared in the answers of sex offenders and controls to this question, that was not the case here. Generally, it was rare for respondents to indicate that scenes from erotica reappeared in their sex fantasies or daydreams.

When this did occur, it was more common for the homosexuals (16% of sample, $p < .01$ vs. controls) to report that the scene they recalled was a segment of homosexual activity. More surprisingly, 14 percent ($p < .07$ vs. controls) of the transsexuals made similar reports while another 14 percent mentioned heterosexual activity of some sort. When users fantasized a theme from erotica, it was predominantly heterosexual.

In table 17, illustrating the number of times that various types of sexual activity were cued off by memories of erotica, the transsexuals stand out in their *low* rate of reported masturbation. Since they do acknowledge an overall rate of masturbation similar to controls, it is masturbation stimulated by erotica that they specifically deny. They indicated repeatedly that masturbating activity was far more likely to be related to self-manufactured erotica in which they either dressed up as the opposite sex, or engaged in sexual relations as a member of the op-

Table 17

REPORTS BY HOMOSEXUALS, TRANSSEXUALS, AND USERS OF SEXUAL
ACTIVITY RELATED TO PRESENCE OR ABSENCE OF EROTICA

Stimuli and Subjects	Never (%)	Few Times (%)	Several Times (%)	Daily (%)	p
Masturbation stimulated by thoughts of erotica					
Homosexuals	31	31	38	0	.02
Transsexuals	83	9	9	0	—
Users	19	25	46	10	.003
Controls	61	14	26	0	—
Masturbation *not* stimulated by erotica					
Homosexuals	14	55	31	0	.004
Transsexuals	33	42	25	0	—
Users	28	49	23	0	.05
Controls	55	32	13	0	—

	Never (%)	Occasionally (%)	Regularly (%)	
How often thoughts of erotica excite person to sexual relations				
Homosexuals	41	32	27	.07
Transsexuals	79	7	14	.02
Users	40	38	21	—
Controls	44	48	7	—
How often thoughts of erotica present *during* sexual relations				
Homosexuals	56	25	18	—
Transsexuals	*	*	*	—
Users	42	25	33	.07
Controls	52	42	5	—

* Transsexuals denied that erotica played any significant role in their sexual lives, so answers to this question are not available for this group.

posite sex. The homosexuals and users however, indicate a higher rate of masturbation than controls, whether or not erotica played a role — reports paralleling those of the institutionalized sex offenders.

Beyond masturbation, how do thoughts of erotica relate to the imitation of sexual relations with others? Once again, the transsexuals are adamant in denying that erotica plays such a role in their lives. One-half of the homosexual sample indicate that erotica does stimulate such imitation. The users, surprisingly, do not differ from controls; erotica does not play a significant role in exciting them to initiate sexual relations with others.

As table 17 indicates, however, the users do stand out in the degree to which thoughts derived from erotica are present in their minds *during* sexual relations. They are the only group in which a substantial number of respondents indicate this to be the case. This means that thoughts or scenes from previously experienced erotica color their actual sexual experiences. ("I'd be making love to my wife and then I'd start thinking she was the girl from that stag film and those thoughts would excite me and make the sex much better.")

Frequency of recent contact with erotica. Respondents were asked how often during the past year they had seen erotica of the type described in their peak experience. There were no significant group differences, although the transsexuals report the lowest rate of recent exposure of all groups.

When asked whether they wanted to obtain some erotica of this type for themselves, almost a third of the controls answered affirmatively (29%). This is a significantly lower percentage than was true for homosexuals (55%, $p < .06$ vs. controls) and users (62%, $p < .005$ vs. controls).

Did the respondents follow through and actually obtain some of their own? Generally, those who wanted to obtain their own erotica did obtain it, and there were no group differences in the percentages of those who did so. When the subsample of respondents who obtained it were asked about quantity, group differences did emerge. Of this subsample (43% and 38% of homosexuals and users, respectively, $p < .03$ and .04 vs. controls), 22 percent were coded as having *many* personal copies of erotica. In this same subsample, the respondents were asked how often they looked at this personal erotica, and, once again, the homosexuals and (to a lesser extent) users stand out from controls (62% and 57%, respectively, of homosexuals and users coded as *regularly* looking at the material, while only 20% of controls who have their own erotica so reported).

Thus, transsexuals stand out from all groups in indicating a lesser desire to obtain their own erotica. Among homosexuals, users, and controls, there are no group differences in desire to obtain erotica, nor in their success in obtaining some. Homosexuals and users, however, are likely to obtain more erotica than controls and to look at it more frequently.

SUMMARY AND CONCLUSIONS

Data on current utilization and impact of erotica suggest that the controls fall between two patterns of response, one characteristic of the homosexuals and users and the other characteristic of the transsexual group.

Both the homosexual and user groups display a heightened sensitivity to the stimulus characteristics of the erotica selected as most vivid, the homosexuals to the aesthetic components and the users to the explicitness of the nudity or sexual activity portrayed. While users and homosexuals do not tend to experiment with new sexual patterns, these groups are highly aroused by erotica and stimulated to engage in sexual relations.

While certain similarities exist between users and homosexuals, the type of erotica selected is in keeping with their respective sexual orientations. Both claim masturbation as a likely consequence of exposure to erotica, homosexuals to homosexual erotica and users to heterosexual erotica. The frequency of masturbation in general, specifically with relation to erotica, is significantly higher than found in the controls, as was true for the sex offender groups. The developmental pattern for controls from adolescence to adulthood represents a decline in masturbatory activity. In all other groups we studied, this decline is much less pronounced.

Unlike the sex offender groups, the homosexuals and users, as adults, do not report reacting to erotica with mixed emotions of arousal and disgust or guilt. Like the controls, they experience sexual arousal via erotica as stimulating and pleasant. The guilt response to erotica, then, is largely confined to those individuals who engage in antisocial patterns of sexual behavior, involving aggression or assault on another.

Other significant differences emerge with regard to the role that erotica plays in contacts with sex partners. In the case of the users and, to a lesser extent, the homosexuals, thoughts of previously experienced erotica are present during sexual contacts and appear to serve a stimulatory function. The users apparently were conditioned to a fantasized representation of sexual arousal during adolescence, and therefore required these images as adjuncts to adult sexual relations. For the controls, by contrast, the sexual partner provided sufficient stimulus for arousal during the sexual act.

The pattern of response for the transsexuals stands at the other end of the continuum from all other groups. They report a limited interest in and contact with erotica as adults. Also, they find that erotica has minimal arousal value, and prefer instead to stimulate themselves by transsexual fantasies and fetishistic objects such as clothing of the opposite sex. Possibly, the low availability of transsexual erotica accounts for this lack of interest.

The low response to erotica reported by transsexuals agrees with the findings of Pomeroy (1969) on a sample of twenty-five male transsexuals. He reports extreme social isolation and a very low level of heterosexual activity throughout the respondents' lives. The limited contact with erotica seems to be a special case of the low heterosexual interest found by Pomeroy. It may be that only after achieving the desired sex status can the transsexual entertain and enjoy sexual fantasies and activity. It would be productive to examine transsexuals' attitudes toward erotica after they have had the sex change operation, to determine if they become more receptive to these symbolic cues.

10

THE ROLE OF FANTASY
IN THE USE OF EROTICA

Some people associate fantasy with absentminded professors who forget where their bicycles are parked or misplace their lecture notes. Others have the impression that fantasy is typical only of eccentrics like Walter Mitty who shuttle between a pleasant, ego-inflating mental world and the all-too-familiar difficulties of the real one. And a few connect fantasy with those seriously disturbed individuals who have forsaken the real world completely and cannot distinguish between reality and the products of their own imaginations. But we are becoming increasingly knowledgeable about individuals as discrete psychological entities, each one a complex pattern of conscious and unconscious drives and wishes. Fantasy is a valuable untapped source of knowledge about the inner workings of the unconscious mind. The quest for self-understanding is enhanced by the use of fantasy as a guide to unexplored areas of the self. We are beginning to understand that fantasy plays an important role in releasing us from the conforming strictures of everyday life and enabling us to experiment with new roles, relationships, ideas, and situations. Fantasy, then, can be valuable in helping us to cope with the problems of everyday life not through escape but through mastery. Sexual fantasies are a logical byproduct of this mental experimentation.

Here we are concerned with the nature and function of sexual fantasy as it relates to actual sexual behavior. Our purpose is to explore the relationship between daydreams, erotic materials, and overt sexual expression. What is the role of fantasy in the sexual lives of our samples? Can it lead us to glimpse something of the unconscious desires of our subjects, or does it function as an escape or coping mechanism for them? Before we present the results of our study, it might be well to briefly discuss some of the previous work done in this area.

Alfred Kinsey and his associates, in their pioneering work on sexual behavior, found that daydreams played an important role in the sexual lives of the subjects they studied (Kinsey et al., 1948, 1953). Most of the males they interviewed used fantasies in their masturbatory activity, and a little less than two-thirds of the females did so. Two percent of those in their female sample were able to reach orgasm just by thinking about erotic situations, without any tactile stimulation at all. Although only about one male in two thousand can achieve orgasm through fantasy alone, nocturnal emissions stimulated by dreams are a common occurrence. These findings alone would suggest that sexual fantasy should be an important area of scientific inquiry.

Although a great deal of scientific investigation has been devoted to night dreams, relatively little work has focused on daydreams and conscious fantasies. Sigmund Freud (1907) stressed the wish-fulfilling nature of daydreams, and in his method of unraveling the unconscious thoughts and feelings of his patients, he utilized daydreams to uncover repressed desires. Work with daydreams remains an important facet of traditional psychotherapy and plays a role in a variety of newer therapies as well. Recent experimental work, especially that of Jerome Singer (1966), has stressed the adaptive and problem-solving function of fantasy. Singer's work brought the subject of daydreaming into the mainstream of general psychological inquiry.

A good deal of work on the role of fantasy in the expression of aggression has direct relevance to the study of erotica. Several researchers have tried to determine whether fantasy aggression diminishes overt aggression or whether seeing or imagining violence prompts one to act aggressively. Feshbach (1961, 1971), in a series of studies, suggested that fantasy served as a cathartic, drive-reducing influence on some individuals. Further studies, especially by Bandura and his associates (1961), imply that fictional representations of aggression are likely to be imitated. In other words, aggression experienced vicariously, through movies or television, could adversely affect the behavior patterns of viewers. Berkowitz (1963), in his investigations into the effects of fantasied violence, concluded that the individual situation determined whether fantasy would be drive-reducing or stimulating. He emphasized the role of guilt in this process.

One can readily see the importance of this controversy for the study of sexual behavior — more specifically, of the effects of erotic materials on overt behavior. Does erotica diminish or encourage the overt expression of sexual wishes? Does erotica provide a relatively harmless outlet for sexual deviants, a kind of safety valve? Or does it stimulate perverse sexual activity in susceptible individuals who would not have been so inflamed without exposure to suggestive material? Everyone has their own theories, and actual public policy is determined by implicit answers to these questions. Let us now turn to the results of our study in regard to fantasy. We cannot presume to give a final definitive answer on the effects of erotica, but we present our data as a first step down a long and complicated path.

RELATIONSHIP BETWEEN THE CONTENT OF SEX FANTASIES
AND SEXUAL BEHAVIOR

Our first concern was to isolate the kinds of sexual daydreams in which our subjects habitually indulged. Each respondent was asked about the content of his sexual daydreams during the year prior to the interview (for sex offenders, the year before institutionalization occurred). We were able to code the results on the following dimensions: most common heterosexual acts; oral-genital activity; homosexual acts; forcible or sadistic acts; and dressing in the clothing of the opposite sex (transvestite acts). The statistical results are presented in table 18.

Most of our samples, as we suspected, did daydream about their sexual activity. Male object pedophiles daydreamed about homosexual activity significantly more than did the controls, and their fantasies contained a high percentage of oral-genital relations. The fantasies of female object pedophiles did not differ greatly from those of our controls. Transsexuals, as one might expect, daydreamed considerably more than other groups about dressing in the clothes of the opposite sex. Confirmed homosexuals daydreamed measurably less about heterosexual intercourse, and more about homosexuality, than the controls. They also engaged in more transvestite fantasies and oral-genital daydreams.

One homosexual related this fantasy: "It's always a homosexual aggressive drive, wishing you could have a child because you love each other. You imagine you're a man and a woman." Another: "My fantasy involves good-looking men in sexual activity." Still others relate more cross-sex fantasies: "Masturbation while imagining I'm wearing women's clothes." "I'm a woman having sex." A man arrested for molesting young boys related that his fantasies were mostly about young boys but added: "I also see myself as a younger boy having sex for the

Table 18
CONTENT OF ADULT DAYDREAMS FOR DEVIANTS AND CONTROLS BY TYPE OF FANTASY ACTIVITY

Fantasy Activity	Rapists	Pedophiles Male	Pedophiles Female	Homosexuals	Transsexuals	Users	Controls
Usual heterosexual							
% yes	90	88.2	90	53.1	83.3	90	79.5
p vs. controls	—	—	—	.03	—	—	—
Homosexual							
% yes	69.2	78.9	26.7	91.2	54.5	50	32.4
p vs. controls	.05	.003	—	.0001	—	—	—
Oral-genital activity							
% yes	83.3	84.2	50	79.4	41.7	85.7	60
p vs. controls	.16	.13	—	.14	—	.02	—
Subject of forcible sadistic acts							
% yes	66.7	16.7	20	20.7	14.3	40.4	30.8
p vs. controls	.02	—	—	—	—	—	—
Transvestite							
% yes	33.3	10	8.3	37	81.8	19.6	8.6
p vs. controls	.11	—	—	.02	.001	—	—

first time with a girl, but it's never come about." This fantasy reflects a wish for more normal sexual relations, even though in his fantasy he makes himself much younger. Similar fantasies, in which the subject engages in more normal activities than he does in real life, are reported by the nonheterosexual samples. Another male object pedophile reported fantasies of "really satisfying" his wife and added that he had a deep fear of never being able to satisfy a woman. Still another felt that some of his fantasies about intercourse were wishful thinking, since his fears of being rejected prevented him from approaching mature women. But most of the fantasies centered on the individuals' deviant activity.

The picture of the rapists, however, is more complex. Rapists predictably report far more fantasies involving forcible or sadistic acts than any other group. But more surprising is the fact that 69 percent of the rapists mention homosexual daydreams, a figure more than double the percentage for controls. The rapists also report more transvestite fantasies and oral-genital daydreams than controls. Thus the rapists seem to be more polymorphous and varied in the range of their sexual fantasies than all other groups. Consider these examples.

One rapist, before his arrest, became obsessed with fantasies about a sadomasochistic relationship in which he was involved: "My fantasy would be about this girl and there would always be whipping, but not to a degree where there would be physical harm. Very rough handling of the breast area and then the sexual act itself. More than a sharing thing, it was an attack."

Another rapist reported that his fantasies were mostly about men: "Well, in my sexual fantasies with men I would masturbate. In my sexual fantasies with women . . . I just felt I don't belong to women. [Question: What was the context?] In general, I would just think about him, what we used to do and how I liked it. [Question: How about your fantasies with women?] I don't know, doctor, I really don't fantasize about women much."

One subject was preoccupied with fantasies about animals as an adolescent, after a girl showed him a book describing sex between a woman and farm animals. The same subject had constant fantasies about intercourse with his daughter.

Still another rapist had fantasies about dressing in his mother's clothes. These fantasies started around the age of five, after he had seen a photo depicting his parents having intercourse. He reports that he fantasized his father's place in the sexual act. The rapist's ambivalent feelings about women are painfully clear in his fantasies about beating or subduing through sex, and in the confusion illustrated by the transvestite fantasy — whether he dresses as a woman or a man. The act of rape may be viewed as an attempt to master feelings of revenge or even helplessness toward women.

The uses individuals make of their erotic daydreams suggest several models of behavior that may clarify the relationship between fantasy and sexual activity. These different models are represented in table 19. One model would postulate a parallel relationship between early childhood experience and choice of erotic depictions of sex in the mass media, conscious daydreams, and overt sexual behavior. Fantasies concerning deviant behavior, for example, dominated the reveries of the pedophile and homosexual samples. Male pedophiles who had been sexually initiated while very young by an older male relative continued to fantasize and also to act out in real life this key experience: "Older fellas would break in guys that were twelve or thirteen. They liked to see guys jackin' off."

But if we return to the data on the rapists, the parallel theory does not clearly explain their many-sided sexual fantasies. This data suggests a second model in which infantile conflicts, erotica, conscious daydreams, and overt sexual behavior are not consistent. Here erotic daydreams may serve a compensatory purpose, warding off other more disturbing fantasies. Or, in some cases, the overt sexual activity of the rape may serve to compensate for the inability to indulge subconscious instincts toward homosexuality, perhaps, or passivity. We shall have more to say about these models later in this chapter.

The users and controls. Our sample of confirmed users of erotic materials reported significantly more daydreams about heterosexual oral-genital activity than did controls, an interest which is consistent with their venturesome attitude toward a variety of sexual experiences. The users demonstrated lively sexual imaginations. "I flash on the scene in *Midnight Cowboy* where Dustin Hoffman dies and the lesbian scene in *Sister George.*" "A woman is making love to me. She's kissing my breasts, my thighs and she's very gentle and her hands are soft like velvet and she has a very feminine soft voice." Another user reported that for him fantasy heightened passion and made sex "sort of a semi-rape." Other users reported fantasies about different partners — a Cuban showgirl, slave girls, an Indian girl from a movie — and different settings — in the grass, in a swimming pool, by a river, and other such places.

One question constituted an invitation to spontaneous creation of fantasy: The users, by and large, came up with the most elaborate responses. Unlike other samples, they did not wish for "the real thing," but rather took advantage of the broad scope of the question. One user wanted "a basement full of sex-starved young nymphs. A harem of

Table 19
RELATIONSHIP BETWEEN FANTASY AND BEHAVIOR: MODELS

	Pornographic Depictions Via Media	Deviant Sexual Behavior
Infantile Conflict ("unconscious fantasy")	a) parallel to childhood history (expressive)	a) parallel to childhood history, choice of pornography, and conscious daydreams
or	b) divergent from childhood history (defensive)	b) divergent from childhood history, choice of pornography, and conscious daydreams
Learned Patterns of Deviant Behavior	Conscious Fantasies; Night Dreams	
	a) parallel to childhood history and choice of pornography	
or	b) divergent from childhood history and choice of pornography	
Childhood Experiences		

beautiful women. Good, graphic photographs of intercourse." Another felt that his preference would be "a stag film with me having intercourse and oral relations with two women. Also women having sex. Something with a woman lying on a bed, completely naked with her legs stretched out, ready to receive a man." Still another would wish the genie to produce "something along the lines of a contemporary Greek or Roman orgy — getting stoned, deep into food, then leading up to sex, a movie." The users' imaginative replies are consistent with their use of erotic material as a sexual stimulus.

In contrast with the fantasies described by users, those reported by our control group usually contained themes of heterosexual intercourse. Some of their more imaginative fantasies were: "I'm just the greatest lover that ever lived. I'm doing everything." "I'm out sailing and balling somebody on a boat." "I fantasize about the most attractive people I've met over the years." "I've got a hangup on busts. Nothing is usually happening. I'm just wishing I could find a big-busted girl." For many of the controls fantasies served to heighten interest with a sex partner who was unresponsive or unattractive. As one control put it: "I only fantasize when I'm with someone I don't like that much."

The Aladdin's lamp question produced some interesting answers from the controls. One subject wanted a "Cinerama version of a girl on a sailboat in a silk or chiffon dress on a sunny day." Another control had a less idyllic request: "A tall redhead, size 42 jugs, measurement 42-26-37, lips like Elke Sommers, in a book." One loyal husband swore that he would request another wife just like the one he had now. Another subject, also thinking along realistic lines, wanted a beautiful woman but added that he could use a magic carpet to transport him to and from the bed. Another wished that the genie could produce his ideal woman — Raquel Welch. He added, revealingly, that he wished her to be made mute so she wouldn't nag him all the time! Finally, one poor soul, perhaps overwhelmed by the possibilities, answered: "I would ask him to make me completely sexless so I wouldn't have to be bothered by it."

So the controls also had fantasies, but they tended to be more mundane and involve heterosexual intercourse, although not necessarily with their present partners.

Fantasies during the sex act. Our control sample reported that 40 percent never daydreamed during sex; 51 percent, sometimes; and 9 percent, always. The female object pedophiles and transsexuals tended to daydream somewhat less than controls and the other samples somewhat more. None of these differences was statistically significant, however.

The subjects were also asked whether they daydreamed during the sex act about their current partner or some other person. Forty-eight percent of the controls answered "my partner" and 41 percent answered "other people." Interestingly, all the sex offenders and nonheterosexual samples reported a higher percentage of fantasies about their partners. Eighty percent of the female object pedophiles in fact fantasied about their partners. Seventy percent of the rapists (p < .05) and 61 percent of the homosexuals reported fantasies about other partners. When we asked the subjects whether these other partners were known to them or not, 17 percent of the controls and 35 percent of the rapists reported unknown partners in their daydreams. Although this is not a statistically significant difference, it is interesting in light of the rapist's basic problem: the impulse to sexually assault unknown women.

The content of the fantasies during intercourse conforms to the regular practices of each sample. The vast majority of the controls, users, rapists, and female object pedophiles imagine heterosexual activity in their daydreams. The pedophiles, male object (56%), homosexuals (91%), and transsexuals (43%) tend to portray homosexual activity. The male object pedophiles portray masturbation significantly more than do the other groups. This masturbation involves the fondling of young boys. It is interesting to note that although the rapists report having homosexual, oral-genital, and other fantasies on occasion, they almost always have fantasies of heterosexual intercourse during the sex act. In fact, 80 percent of their fantasies contain only themes of heterosexual intercourse, a much higher percentage than that for the controls (56%, p < .10). This suggests still another compensatory mechanism on the part of the rapist, by which he tries to ward off sadistic or other unwanted fantasies during intercourse.

The subjects were asked whether they found daydreaming more exciting before or during the sex act. The controls answered: 57 percent before, 21 percent during, and 21 percent neither. The rapists (77%) and the male object pedophiles (71%) found daydreaming more exciting before. Perhaps their fantasies play a part in stimulating them to sustain the sexual act. The transsexuals (40%) found fantasies during sex most exciting. Perhaps the sex act itself promoted their fantasies of actually being a woman.

We can speculate on the function of fantasy during the sexual act. For some, it may serve to heighten arousal with a partner who is unattractive or unenthused. At a deeper level, perhaps the fantasies serve to maintain potency for individuals who may be anxious about the sexual encounter. Thus, fantasies of other than the one who is present, or unfamiliar partners, may be exciting as a source not only of arousal but of anxiety reduction about sex with the real partner. This anxiety may be unconscious, and the fantasy keeps it that way.

It is important to note again that the rapists have ordinary daydreams during the sexual act, but varied and perverse daydreams at other times. This finding is consistent with our earlier idea that fantasy can serve a compensatory and defensive as well as expressive function.

Relationship between fantasies and preferred type of pornography. The data we have presented on fantasy content raises an intriguing question concerning the relationship between one's daydreams and the type of erotica one finds most exciting. The subjects were asked whether they were able to find erotic materials that vividly portrayed their regular sex daydreams. Forty-eight percent of the controls said that they had. Over half of the other groups answered affirmatively with figures slightly higher than the controls. But an unusually high percentage (78%, p < .001) of the users so reported, a finding that is consistent with their rich and varied fantasy life. For the users, then, there seems to be a direct and important connection between their daydreams and their use of erotica.

Another focus of interest is the content of the daydreams and the content of the exciting erotica. One might expect that the content of sexual daydreams would parallel the erotica that is most stimulating. The homosexuals we studied, for example, daydreamed about homosexual activity, often involving oral-genital relations. The type of erotica that they found most appealing as "peak experiences" often involved homosexual content similar to that in their daydreams. The case of the rapist is quite different, however, as the data given below suggests.

In an honors thesis, Gillette (1971) carefully matched our sample of twenty rapists with twenty controls of the same age, educational level, marital status, and area of residence (for rapists before arrest). The most vivid and exciting experience in adolescence and adulthood was taken as a measure of preferred type of erotica. These "peak experiences" were coded on the following dimensions: nude women, heterosexual intercourse, oral-genital activity, male homosexuality, female homosexuality, sadomasochism, group sex, and no reported pornography. The results are shown in table 20.

There were no significant differences in the content of the material rapists and controls found most exciting in either adolescence or adulthood. Heterosexual activity was the focus of the "peak experience" for both groups at these two stages of their lives. One rapist reported that sadomasochistic activity comprised his peak experience with erotica during his teen years; two rapists reported this material as most exciting in their most recent experience. None of the controls reported sadomasochistic content in their peak teen or recent experiences. The rapists' reports of sadomasochism are far fewer than we might have expected.

Erotic Material	Rapists (%)			Controls (%)			p
	Teen	Adult	T	Teen	Adult	T	
Nude women	15	55	35	25	55	40	—
Heterosexual relations	50	20	35	55	30	42.5	—
Oral-genital	5	0	2	0	0	0	—
Male homosexuality	0	0	0	0	0	0	—
Lesbians	10	5	7.5	0	5	2.5	—
Sadomasochism	5	10	7.5	0	0	0	—
Group sex	5	0	2.5	10	0	5	—
No reported pornography	10	10	10	10	10	10	—

One clue to this finding lies in the attitude that our sample of rapists has toward sadomasochistic material. They reported far more disgust toward these materials than did the controls $(p > .09)$. Perhaps the rapists prefer ordinary heterosexual themes in their erotica to avoid the unpleasant feelings of guilt and disgust sadomasochistic material might generate.

Most of the experiences with erotica reported as most exciting by the rapists involved watching nude women in topless or bottomless bars or seeing pictures of them in magazines, with heterosexual themes involved in both cases. One man talked about a movie he saw in which Elizabeth Taylor took off her clothes while trying to entice her husband into bed. What stood out in his mind was that the husband had second thoughts about her proposal! Although this movie had a clear heterosexual theme, the scene the rapist remembered is a key indication of his own ambivalence toward seductive women.

Another rapist talked about an experience in a topless bar he frequented with male friends: "This girl had on a miniskirt and she didn't have any underwear on and everyone was standing there with matches and lighters trying to see. Someone would put a dollar on top of the bar and she would come over and the guy would ogle at her. It was something different from the run-of-the-mill topless bars. Topless bars get boring unless I went with a bunch of guys. I couldn't see going in myself." Again, the content is explicitly heterosexual, but the necessity of going with "a bunch of guys" seems to reflect the subject's uneasiness about seeing boldly seductive women.

For other rapists, outstanding erotica included the nudes in *Playboy,* a large advertisement showing a naked woman, a girl pulling off her G-string in a burlesque, or belly dancers. One rapist mentioned a psychology textbook dealing with incest as his most exciting recent experience with erotic materials!

What is significant about these data is that none of the rapists reports homosexual erotica as being most exciting in adolescence or adulthood. Further, oral-genital activity was rarely the outstanding experience with erotica, particularly in comparison with our other samples. These findings suggest a difference between the content of rapists' conscious daydreams (homosexuality, transvestism, oral-genital activity) and the content of erotica they found most exciting. Our conclusion is that the rapists' choice of conventional erotica may be defensive in the sense that it reduces the importance of the other more perverse fantasies they report imagining in daydreams.

Another question raised by these findings concerns the effect of this "screening" process — weeding out perverse erotica in favor of more standard material — for the rapists. Does this process keep them from acting out their more dangerous fantasies? For our sample, at any rate, it would appear that erotic materials do not substitute effectively for the violent activities that fulfill their sexual needs. It is as if they attempt to use the material to ward off their perverse impulses, but with minimal success.

Incorporation of erotic material in daydreams. In previous chapters, data have been presented which show the degree to which our samples borrowed from sexual materials themes for their own daydreams, during adolescence and in their recent experience. These data will be briefly reviewed here, to place them in the context of our present focus on fantasy. A high percentage of all samples reported that they did use scenes from erotica in their own daydreams during adolescence. Two users' comments are typical. "Before I started heterosexual activity I used to masturbate looking at pictures." "I remember flashing back to the scene in *Candy* where she has intercourse with the hunchback." Among the noninstitutionalized samples, the confirmed users were more likely and the transsexuals less likely to incorporate scenes from erotica in their adolescent daydreams.

Of the sex offender groups, a significantly large percentage of rapists said that they used erotica in their teen-age daydreams. It was also the rapists who were the most likely to report that their recurring sexual daydreams incorporated aspects of sexual techniques or characters from the erotic materials they had seen in adolescence.

Similar questions were asked concerning the subjects' most recent adult experiences. Few controls found in erotica source material for their recent adult sexual reveries. The rapists, however, reported incorporating depictions of heterosexual intercourse in their daydreams significantly more than the controls. The pedophiles, male objects, incorporated themes of homosexual oral-genital relations in their fantasies. This statement from a molester of boys serves as illustration. "I was always thinking about sex with boys. I didn't get a good feeling when having sex with a girl. In these pictures I saw a man giving another a blowjob. It started me going to adults and later I went back to children. . . . It just put me back into childhood." The homosexual and transsexual samples, as might be expected, incorporated more homosexual themes from the erotica they used than did the controls.

The reader will recall that the rapists stand out as the only group reporting significant negative emotions when the scenes from erotica appeared in their daydreams. This pattern of arousal and disgust was found in both the teen-age and adult experience of the rapist.

What is important here is that the rapists report no utilization of sadomasochistic, oral-genital, or homosexual themes from erotica in their daydreams. This means that they may be using the erotic material to incorporate heterosexual themes into their fantasies to offset the guilt-arousing content of the perverse thoughts generated in their own heads. Even the scenes from erotica, when incorporated as part of the rapists' own fantasies, are regarded with disgust.

Erotica, daydreams, and overt sexual expression. The crucial questions in our research on erotica concern the role of such material in stimulating direct sexual expression. Does the use of erotica lead directly or even indirectly to action, and especially to deviant action? This extremely complex question may never be answered satisfactorily, but our study suggests certain tentative conclusions.

The subjects were asked whether their partners used erotica to arouse *them* sexually. Very few of the controls reported that erotica was used by their partners in sexual activity. The male object pedophiles and the homosexuals report erotica as a significant part of their partners' sexual behavior with them (< .01 vs. controls).

The subjects were asked about the ways in which they used erotica to arouse themselves. On the one hand, all the sex offenders and non-heterosexual groups, except the transsexuals, report more use of erotica in connection with heightening pleasure before or during masturbation, rather than before or during sexual intercourse. The controls, on the other hand, when they used erotica for arousal, usually did so in connection with intercourse.

Subjects were also asked whether erotic materials aroused them to masturbation in their current sexual life. The results, presented in previous chapters, indicate that all the sex offenders and nonheterosexual groups, again except for the transsexuals, were far more likely to be aroused to masturbation by erotica than were the controls. Other data indicated that these individuals masturbated far more often than the controls without the stimulus of erotica, suggesting that there is not necessarily a causal connection between the amount of masturbation and the use of erotica. Rather, it seems that the masturbation aroused by erotica is part of a larger pattern of masturbatory activity, activity which is a great deal more frequent in sex offenders and nonheterosexual groups than in the control sample.

We have also presented data dealing with the role of erotica in arousing the subjects to intercourse. No statistically significant differences were found between our control and other samples in this regard. It should be noted that the rapists, pedophiles with male objects, homosexuals, and users were aroused to intercourse in greater percentages than the controls, particularly the rapists.

Our findings do not show a direct connection between the use of erotica and overt sexual expression. For most of our sex offenders and nonheterosexual samples, the use of erotica is associated with masturbation. But this masturbation is so pervasive that a causal link seems not to be present. The data with regard to intercourse points up the stimulating effect that pornography has on some noncontrol samples (e.g., homosexuals), but the percentages are not high enough to warrant any definitive conclusions. More careful research into the vulnerability of certain groups or individuals to sexual stimuli is needed. Rapists, for example, seem to be flooded with sexual fantasies, and they incorporate aspects of erotica into these fantasies. It would seem that these fantasies might well have more to do with triggering actual behavior rather than the erotic materials that the rapists seem to use to ward off their more disturbing daydreams.

SUMMARY AND CONCLUSIONS

We would like to conclude with some general thoughts about daydreams and erotic materials. In our view erotic pictures, stories, and movies simply serve as a substitute for the self-generating daydreams of the pornography user. The erotic appeal of pornographic materials stems from their connection with the user's inner fantasies.

But the daydream and erotic pictures are really two different types of fantasy activity. The daydream comes apparently from some inner stimulation to one's imagination. In the case of erotica, the theme portrayed comes from someone else's imagination, is depicted in tangible form, and can be thought of as separate from one's own wishes and motivations. This difference can be quite important psychologically. In this chapter we have explored the relationship between our subjects' conscious daydreams and the fantasies portrayed in the type of erotic materials they use.

Our study of the use of erotica by sex offenders and nonheterosexuals suggests several models of behavior that may clarify the function of erotica as fantasy. Psychoanalytic theory has postulated that erotic fantasies (both day and night dreams) may be considered psychic representations of early infantile conflicts, long repressed by the individual's subconscious. These fantasies may parallel the actual childhood events, or may be unrealistic versions of the real events. In this light, antisocial sexual activity may be seen as the active response to remnants of unresolved infantile conflict. For example, the act of rape may be viewed as an attempt to master feelings of revenge or even passive helplessness with regard to women, feelings that may have originated in the rapist's childhood, but of which he is not consciously aware.

Other data on fantasy usage support this hypothesis linking erotic fantasies, childhood conflict, and adult behavior. One type of fantasy usage involves a parallel relationship between choice of erotic depictions in media, conscious daydreams, and sexual behavior. For example, a sadist will choose depictions of sadistic pornography and will have sadistic fantasies. A similar parallel is sometimes discovered between childhood events and the choice of erotic material. Robert Stoller (1970) describes a fascinating case of a transvestite who was particularly excited by an erotic story involving a young man who is forced by powerful females to dress in the clothes of the opposite sex, an exact parallel of this transvestite's personal history as a child. We can call this use of erotica *expressive* in that the choice of pornography expresses a fantasy that parallels childhood events and adult behavior. This expressive function of fantasy, in which daydreams, erotica, and overt behavior seemed consistent in thematic content, was exemplified in our male object pedophile, homosexual, and transsexual samples. The female object pedophiles reported a fantasy life similar to that of the controls.

The function of erotica for our sample of confirmed users, and to some extent for our controls, could be termed expressive also. In their choice of erotica the users found an outlet for their suppressed desires to experience heterosexual oral-genital behavior and similar activities.

The same can be said of the controls. Fantasy was used to heighten arousal and thus can be said to have had an expressive function.

Another function of fantasy seems to be that of disguising conscious or unconscious fantasies even more productive of anxiety and guilt. In this case, the individual's choice of erotica, conscious daydreams, and overt sexual preference is not consistent and parallel. We can call this use of fantasy *defensive,* in that it serves a compensatory function, having more to do with anxiety and guilt than sexual drive. This defensive approach is common among the rapists. They reported oral-genital, homosexual, and transvestite daydreams, as well as fantasies involving aggression and sadism — themes that disgust and upset them — in greater profusion than did the controls. This contrasts sharply with their reports that the erotica they find most stimulating involves depictions of simple heterosexual intercourse. Similarly, their rapist behavior conflicts with their nonheterosexual daydreams.

This kind of analysis suggests that the study of the use of erotica by sex offenders can lead to a better understanding of their psychological makeup. For the rapist, his overt preoccupation with force and violence stands in contrast with his conscious daydreams that involve oral-genital relations, homosexuality, and dressing in the clothes of the opposite sex. His frequent masturbation, his feelings of inadequacy with regard to winning women, also reflect his sexual difficulties, which he attempts to resolve by the act of rape.

A description by one rapist coincides with this analysis: "Hiding and waiting for the girl to walk along at night and thinking of doing a lot of things I was too scared to do when I actually did it." The things? "It was a real hurried thing. It would be a real brief intercourse and just run. I'd fantasize why didn't I stay there fifteen or twenty minutes and have more complete intercourse. . . . Caress her, oral-copulate with her, and her oral-copulate me, caress her a lot more, having her reach climax." He speaks wistfully of what he would like to do with women if only they would yield to his demands. The rapist, in his preferences in erotica, is trying to assert his "normality" but perverse fantasies constantly intrude and disturb this resolve.

Stoller's transvestite case, mentioned above, is another illustration of the usefulness of erotica as an area of investigation. Bell and Hall (1971) studied another form of fantasy — manifest night dreams — to illuminate the personality of a pedophile. In our research, we found that the choice of erotica and conscious sexual daydreams of the users yielded a great deal of information about their personalities. In general, we can conclude that analysis of the use of erotica and sexual fantasy can be a valuable tool for understanding sexual behavior.

We return now to the focus of this chapter: Is fantasy a stimulating or cathartic agent in antisocial sexual behavior? Our data suggest that a simple answer to this question does not exist. But let us review the findings of our study.

There is no evidence in our data to suggest that erotica per se triggers antisocial sexual behavior. Sex offenders do utilize scenes from erotica in their daydreams; rapists are especially prone to do so. The use of erotica stimulates some sex offenders and nonheterosexuals to masturbate more frequently than controls. These groups, however, masturbate more frequently than the controls in general. There were no significant differences between controls and the other samples regarding the role of sexual materials in stimulating sexual intercourse. The use of erotica seems to be part of a larger fantasy sexual life, and the masturbation associated with erotica part of a larger pattern of masturbatory behavior.

It would seem that the rapist is beset with a variety of self-generated fantasies, which he finds distasteful but which he cannot control. Rather than being cathartic, these daydreams apparently lead him further toward action. Pornography, however, is neither stimulating nor cathartic, instead serving as a means of warding off anxiety, disgust, and guilt about his disturbing daydreams.

Further research is definitely needed on the role of conscious daydreams as a contributing factor in sexual offenses. This kind of investigation, focusing on the individual's entire fantasy life and not simply on erotica, would seem to be the most fruitful in terms of assessing the relationship between fantasy and criminal sexuality.

We found that the study of our subjects' fantasies was an excellent means of increasing our understanding of them and of the role erotic materials play in their lives. It is for future researchers to analyze more systematically the link between erotic fantasies, self-generated or otherwise, and human sexual behavior. Sigmund Freud once said that dreams were the royal road to man's unconscious mind. We hope it is not too bold to state that the study of erotica may be a bumpy back road to that same destination.

*I do not have the professional interest
of social scientists in the academic aspects of whether or not
obscenity is the direct cause of every antisocial act
committed by a person "addicted to" or the "reader"
of such materials. It is enough for me that
a relationship has been found. On this matter
my contacts with law enforcement officers
over the past thirteen years
have confirmed what my own
intelligence tells me is so.*

CHARLES H. KEATING,
Minority Report, U.S. Commission on Obscenity and Pornography

11

PSYCHOLOGICAL IMPLICATIONS
OF THE STUDY

The varieties of data presented in the previous chapters suggest a number of trends worthy of further study, as follows:

1. Controls, sexual offenders, and nonheterosexuals reported an equivalent amount of exposure to erotica during their preadolescent years. The material encountered typically involved nudity, but depictions of sexual activity were rare.

2. Controls differed from all other groups in the degree of exposure to erotica during adolescence: they generally experienced more of it, in more explicit forms. The sharpest differences were noted in the extent of their encounters with symbolic representation of what our culture terms the "normal" sex act — heterosexual intercourse.

3. All groups reported a marked degree of arousal from erotica as teen-agers. This erotica stimulated sexual fantasies, but little overt sexual behavior, aside from masturbation.

4. All groups reported a significant amount of information about sexual relations garnered from erotica encountered during adolescence. This information typically involved information about the anatomy of the opposite sex and patterns of heterosexual relations.

5. The sex offender groups, in particular, reported a pattern of re-

sponse to erotica found in people identified as high in sex guilt, which was not true for the control sample.

6. In adult life, the sex offender groups continued to report less frequent exposure to erotica than controls. This was not true for the homosexual and user samples, who exceeded the frequency of exposure to erotica reported by controls.

7. While frequency of exposure in adulthood was less for sex offenders, its impact was very similar to that reported for adolescence. Arousal and masturbation were still part of the sexual pattern of these groups, while the controls sought appropriate heterosexual outlets when aroused by erotica.

8. Generally, erotic materials function as a substitute for the user's self-generated daydreams, and resemble those daydreams in content.

9. Two models of the relationship between the type of erotica selected, conscious daydreams, and sexual behavior emerged. One emphasized the use of erotica as *expressive* of conscious fantasies, while the other is *defensive* and used to ward off unacceptable desires. The latter was particularly characteristic of the rapist sample.

So far, in this book, we have not considered sources of bias, either in sampling or method of data collection, that could invalidate these nine general conclusions. What artifacts of procedure might there have been in our study which limit the applicability of the findings?

How sound were our methods? We have, of course, based a great deal upon interviews with individuals, intensive interviews with numerous builtin cross-checks. These cross-checks frequently corrected inaccurate information, as when negative answers concerning exposure to a particular type of erotica were negated by an affirmative reply to a subsequent variant of the same question. The range of questions and the cross-checks did appear adequate to stimulate recall of earlier experiences and to enhance the validity of replies. Naturally, we were not in a position either to elicit deeply repressed experiences of early childhood or preadolescence, or to estimate the potential bias in our results from these subconscious memories. It has been our observation, contrary to our expectations, that experiences with erotica, because they are vivid and highly charged, are readily retrieved in considerable detail. We were constantly amazed at the thoroughness of our respondents' descriptions of plot, theme, drawings, or photos from their preadolescence and teen-age years. These data do not suggest that the findings that set the controls apart from the sex offender groups are based upon variations in the ability to recall experience with erotica during earlier periods of life.

There is another, more subtle type of bias that must be considered in attempting to evaluate our findings. Could there be some vested interest, not present in the control sample, that might motivate the sex offenders and nonheterosexuals to be less than candid in describing their early exposure to erotica? For example, might the sexual offenders play down their degree of exposure to erotica in order to emphasize their psychological health, or emphasize that exposure in an attempt to blame their sex offense on some external agent such as pornography? It is not inconceivable, but the evidence seems to indicate otherwise. First, the interviews with the sex offenders, and to a lesser extent the nonheterosexual and user samples, were significantly longer than the interviews with the controls — primarily because the responses of the former groups were more extensive. This suggests that the noncontrol groups were not actively defensive or censorious of their replies. Second, the replies of the noncontrol groups contained material of a highly personal nature in which details of intimate, and in the case of sex offenders rather morbid, fantasies and desires were readily revealed. Thus it seems unlikely that their generally low level of reported experiences with erotica might be part of a general set to inhibit personally meaningful reports of sexual desires or behavior. In fact, interviewers found that it was most difficult to elicit full and detailed reports of sexual experiences from the control sample.

Since most of the data do suggest that the controls stand apart from all the other groups studied, it is entirely possible that through some quirk of sample *they* represent the deviant group, while the other groups reflect the attitudes and experiences common to the general population. A number of factors make this argument a plausible one. First, we indicated in chapter 4 that the match between controls and certain of the other groups was inexact with regard to age and education levels. Second, only a portion of those selected for the control study from the door-to-door canvassing of potential respondents actually agreed to be interviewed.

Fortunately, we do have available data from some other studies carried out for the Commission on Obscenity and Pornography (1970) that bear on this issue. A public opinion survey of a national sample, selected on a probability basis to be representative of the total United States male population, included a number of the questions contained in our interview, concerning degree of exposure to erotica during adolescence. Similar studies were carried out with different control populations. Table 21 indicates the percent of respondents in each of these samples who reported *any* experience with erotic books or erotic pictures during their adolescent years. Included in the table are the findings from our samples of white and black "ghetto" controls, which coincide closely with those of the National Opinion Survey (Abelson et al., 1970) for males twenty-one to twenty-nine years old. Of our white controls, 80 percent and 85 percent respectively reported adolescent ex-

Table 21
EXTENT OF EXPOSURE AMONG DELINQUENT
AND NONDELINQUENT YOUTH*

Population	Erotic† Books (%)	Erotic† Pictures (%)
Incarcerated delinquents, 17–20 years (Propper, 1970)	77	84
National sample, males 18–20 years, living in parents' home (Abelson et al., 1970)	68	63
National sample, males 21–29 years (Abelson et al., 1970)	82	81
National sample, college students, 17–24 years (Berger, Simon and Gagnon, 1970)	88	95
Urban working-class high school students, juniors and seniors (Elias, 1970)	95	81
Urban working-class adolescents, 13–18 years (Berger, Simon and Gagnon, 1970)	79	77
Los Angeles working-class white males reporting on their adolescent experience (Goldstein et al., 1970)	80	85
Los Angeles black "ghetto" males reporting on their adolescent experience (Goldstein et al., 1970)	81	78

* "Extent" refers to the proportion of a given population reporting any experience with erotic material.
† Refers to depictions of heterosexual intercourse.

posure to erotic books and erotic pictures depicting sexual intercourse. The comparable figures for the national probability sample are 82 percent and 81 percent respectively. Also, the data from the individuals in our white and black control samples, who varied markedly in average age and educational levels, do not vary at all. Thus it seems unlikely, based on the limited basis for comparison among independent samples, that our controls differ significantly from other more systematically collected control samples.

The next issue, whether our sex offender, nonheterosexual, and user samples are biased representatives of their respective populations, is also worthy of consideration. In the case of the sex offenders, we have previously indicated (see chapter 4) that our samples are highly representative, in terms of demographic criteria, of sex offenders hospitalized in the state of California. They also conform reasonably closely to the characteristics of sex offenders in the Gebhard et al. study (1965). And other studies carried out for the pornography commission found similar trends of less-than-average exposure to erotica in sex offender samples that differed from ours in other respects. Thus, our sex offender samples need not be considered atypical.

The samples of homosexuals, transsexuals, and users pose different problems in estimating bias, as we cannot estimate the characteristics of the total population from which they were drawn. Clearly, they are more willing than most nonheterosexuals and pornography users to talk about themselves; but we do not know how closely their data parallels the trends for the "silent majority" of homosexuals, transsexuals, and users. We might conclude that these samples would be more likely to report heavy contact with erotica in adulthood, when their sexual identities have been confirmed. But, while this was true for the homosexual sample, the transsexuals reported a very low degree of exposure to erotica as adults.

When we consider the methods of data collection and the comparison with data from other independent samples of sex offenders and controls, there is no strong evidence that our findings are the result of major distortions in procedure or sampling. It is always possible that some subtle bias, not obvious to someone intimately connected with the study, might account for the differences found among our groups. Perhaps the best checks against bias in social science research are replications of data by independent investigations on different samples. Since these have been largely confirmatory of the trends reported in this book, we feel that our findings possess generality.

CHILDHOOD EXPERIENCES AND RESPONSE TO EROTICA

In the hope that the backgrounds of our respondents might help explain the role of pornography in their lives, we looked for differences in their childhood experiences. These data were collected as the final sections of the clinical interviews, using a closed-end format. The findings for each group are summarized below.

Rapists. The rapists, who found it very difficult to talk about sex, said that there was little nudity in their homes while they were growing up and that sex was never discussed. Only 18 percent of the rapists said their parents had caught them with erotic materials; in those instances the parents had become angry and had punished them. (In the control group, 37 percent reported that their parents knew they read erotic materials, but only 7 percent reported being punished. Most said that their parents had been indifferent, and some said their parents had explained the materials to them — an occurrence not reported by any other group.)

Rapists tended to oppose premarital sex, and many of them relied on their wives for a great deal of their sex information. This may indicate late learning, a supposition supported by an Atascadero staff member who told us that sex offenders frequently display great ignorance of sexual matters. He said that at least one rapist, when he was first admitted to the hospital, had had no idea where babies come from. Rapists cited extensive extramarital intercourse and a high frequency of sexual relations, but they also reported less enjoyment of sex and more homosexual experience than controls.

Pedophiles. Male object pedophiles found talking about sex more uncomfortable than any other group. There had been little tolerance of nudity in their childhood homes, and no discussion of sex. Male friends were the main source of their sex information.

Most had never married and they were opposed to premarital sex. As we had expected, they were more tolerant of homosexuality than were the controls. Fifty percent of this group had had their first homosexual experiences before they were fourteen, and had learned about masturbation from friends rather than through self-discovery. They rarely reported steady sex partners, and they said that when they did have intercourse, it tended to be unsatisfying.

Female object pedophiles also reported little discussion of sex in their childhood homes. Male friends gave them little of their sex information, and they had learned significantly more about sex from clergymen than controls had. They, too, were uncomfortable in talking about sex, and were the least permissive of all groups regarding premarital and extramarital intercourse. Most had been married. A relatively high number in this group (31%) had had their first sexual experiences with prostitutes.

Homosexuals. Homosexuals reported less permissive attitudes toward nudity in their childhood homes than controls, but this shifted in teenage years toward greater permissiveness. They obtained less sex information from their fathers than did controls, and proportionately more from their mothers (also true of pedophile, male object group), and they learned less about sex from female friends than controls. Unlike the institutionalized sex offenders, 100 percent of the homosexuals reported complete comfort in talking about sex during the interview, and had no reservations about homosexuality as a mode of sexual expression. They express highly liberal attitudes regarding premarital and extramarital relations. As with the pedophiles, male object group, 32 percent reported having their first homosexual experience by age fourteen. They began to masturbate at an early age and learned about it through self-discovery. They had fewer steady sex partners than controls and were more likely to have attended an orgy recently. A high percentage found their sexual relations satisfactory.

Transsexuals. Unlike sex offenders and homosexuals, they reported a fair amount of nudity displayed in their childhood home, becoming less frequent in their teen-age years. Sex was more frequently a topic of conversation in the home than with other noncontrol groups. Unlike all other groups, these male transsexuals report learning more about sex from their sisters than the controls. They also learned more from physicians, perhaps in search of information regarding their sex role confusion. Only 70 percent of this group expressed the opinion that homosexuality was acceptable. The transsexuals are also less permissive concerning premarital sex than homosexuals, with 15 to 20 percent believing it to be absolutely wrong. Eighteen percent of transsexuals report never having had heterosexual intercourse. Generally, transsexuals reported little premarital sexual experience of any kind. Few have a steady sex partner, and those who did have one recently reported a low rate of sexual activity. Less than one-third of the transsexuals report that heterosexual intercourse was a pleasant experience for them. Most rate sexual activity as unsatisfying.

Users. Frequent users of pornography felt more comfortable when talking about sex than the sex offender groups did. Their parents had taken permissive attitudes toward nudity in the home while they were children, although as they had reached adolescence parental attitudes had become less tolerant. When their parents became aware of their children's interest in erotic materials, they showed little concern and did not punish them.

Users had liberal sexual attitudes; over 75 percent approved of premarital sex and took a tolerant view of homosexuality. They tended to have had first intercourse later than most other groups, and a considerable number had had sexual intercourse first with prostitutes. Adultery was more common in this group, and many members had had more than seven extramarital affairs. They had intercourse about as often as controls did, but they used a wider variety of means to reach orgasm (petting, oral stimulation, oral-genital stimulation) than the controls. Users of pornography reported that they enjoyed sex greatly .

RELATIONSHIPS OF EARLY EXPERIENCE, SEXUAL ATTITUDES,
AND RESPONSE TO EROTICA

For the *rapists,* the data suggest very repressive family backgrounds regarding sexuality. The pattern of inhibition and punitiveness in their

families appears to be consistent with rapists' reports of extensive heterosexual and homosexual activity with little enjoyment. They give "fear
of sex" as a reason to explain why pornography does not stimulate them
to engage in or even to desire sexual activity. Rapists are less likely than
controls to encounter sadomasochistic pornography, so the idea for
the aggressive sexual act does not appear to derive from pornography.
A high percentage of rapists report frequent homosexual activity, which
suggests that the aggressive heterosexual rape may sometimes represent
an attempt to deny homosexual tendencies.

Molesters of boys tend to be sexually immature at the time of their first
homosexual contacts. Their low exposure to erotica suggests that their
sexual development was influenced more by actual childhood sexual
contacts than by erotica.

Molesters of girls appear to have developed highly restrictive attitudes
that interfere with their ability to attain or to enjoy mutual sexual relations. Given their restrictive and intolerant attitudes toward premarital
sex, it seems reasonable to suppose that they associate sex with sin and
perversion. Perhaps their choice of immature girls represents a search
for sex partners who are ignorant of sexual matters, and therefore
"innocent."

In contrast with controls, the *homosexuals* and *users* shifted their
position markedly from adolescence to adulthood. The lesser exposure
for these groups during adolescence, and the increasing exposure in their
adult years, differ sharply from control reports. It appears that the homosexuals show an obsessive interest in homosexual erotica, and the
users in both heterosexual and homosexual erotica. The pattern for the
homosexual suggests a high sensitivity to and awareness of sexual stimuli in general. It is very likely that his marked interest in homosexual
erotica reflects an active involvement in the "homosexual community"
(Hooker, 1962) typical of members of a homophile organization such
as One, Incorporated. Coleman (1964) suggests that "where the homosexual has become affiliated with an organized homosexual group, there
is a tendency for him to think of his problem as a group problem. . . .
In such cases, there may be little feeling of fear or conflict and the individual may accept his homosexual behavior as a perfectly natural form
of sexual expression; he may even take pride in his homosexual behavior
and consider himself 'emancipated' from conventional heterosexual
morality." Possibly one way to demonstrate emancipation is to encounter, as often as possible, homosexual erotica. Since our data are
based upon a sample of homosexuals willing to join a homophile organization and to be publicly identified with this sex role, it is difficult to

know whether the trends found also apply to the "silent majority" of homosexuals not willing to be publicly identified.

The users do not ordinarily belong to some organized subculture in society, so their behavior cannot be interpreted in these terms. Clearly, their adult actions suggest a compensatory interest in erotica following limited adolescent exposure, coupled with the broadest range of sexual practices of all groups. They seem motivated to experience heterosexual relations in all possible ways, either symbolically through pornography or actively, through their current sexual contacts. When asked about their sex attitudes and practices, users emerged as generally permissive but their first heterosexual intercourse was usually experienced when they were somewhat older than other groups. Thus, while sexual interest and curiosity were tolerated, they had limited exposure to erotica and went through the greater part of their adolescence without experiencing heterosexual intercourse. Two possible explanations suggest themselves, both of which may apply. First, the users' extensive interest in all varieties of sexuality may represent an attempt to "make up for lost time." Second, high parental tolerance of sexual activity, little contact with erotica, and little sexual experience may permit certain infantile fantasies concerning sexuality to persist into adulthood, so that, with greater opportunity for sexual expression, they color the experiences desired. These hypotheses are also consistent with the users' reported high rate of masturbation associated with erotic stimuli, especially as adults. This erotica-masturbation cycle may be part of the effort to compensate for lost social sexual opportunities through fantasies and self-stimulation.

Functions of erotica. It appears that all our noncontrol groups, no matter what their ages, education, or occupations, share one common characteristic: they had little exposure to erotica when they were adolescents. This suggests that a reasonable degree of exposure to erotica, particularly during adolescence, reflects a high degree of sexual interest and curiosity that correlates with adult patterns of acceptable heterosexual practice. Less-than-average adolescent exposure to pornography reflects either avoidance of heterosexual stimuli, or development in a restrictive and punitive atmosphere. It appears that the amount of exposure to pornography is a surface manifestation of the total pattern of sexual development. If an individual's sexual development is proceeding along a deviant track, then his exposure to pornography will be either minimal or excessive.

It appears that unresolved adolescent sexual conflicts relate to adult sexual patterns that require erotica as a necessary stimulus to gratification. In most heterosexual males, the adolescent use of erotica declines and the sexual partner becomes the primary source of arousal and gratification. A similar point was made by Drs. Morris Lipton and Edward D. Greenword, members of the Obscenity Commission, in one of a series of separate statements made by commission members. They suggest that the varieties of studies carried out for the commission might be interpreted using an analogy based on the process of immunization in biology.

It appears well-established that sexual interests are instinctually derived and that they are present from infancy through old age with different degrees of intensity. Consequently, it is impossible to fully protect children from exposure to sexual stimuli. From the dirty words of the six-year-old to the graffiti present in the toilets of schools and public buildings to the "dirty" stories and pictures of the teen-ager, it would appear that exposure is omnipresent. One may, therefore, ask whether such an exposure may not be an inevitable part of growing up in any culture and whether it may even serve a purpose. Gradual and age-appropriate exposure to erotic stimuli may lead to the development of socially appropriate defense mechanisms like sublimation, repression, postponement and self control. Although the analogy may be somewhat far-fetched, it seems possible that graded exposure may immunize in somewhat the same fashion that exposure to bacteria and viruses builds resistance. If this analogy has merit, total lack of exposure would render the child who is totally unexposed as helpless as the animal raised in a totally sterile environment. That sex offenders tend to come from highly restricted families and have had less than the usual exposure to erotica suggests that they may not have had the opportunity to develop appropriate self control.

To continue the analogy, overwhelming exposure might cause illness rather than immunization. An especially vulnerable period is likely following puberty when sexual impulses of increasing intensity emerge. A major problem of adolescence is that of impulse control, and in our troubled and rapidly changing world youngsters are already hyperstimulated. To add to this stimulation by a completely permissive attitude with respect to the availability of sexual materials appears imprudent. For this reason, we have voted for the juvenile legislation.

We agree with this statement that the functions of erotica vary with the developmental stage of the viewer. In adolescence erotica appears to serve multiple and complex functions. It stimulates the teen-ager's emerging sexual curiosity, and provides concrete models of the actual "mechanics" of heterosexual relationships. Unfortunately, our data indicate that erotica is often the only media through which this specific information is gained. Reactions to this information concerning the anatomy of sexual organs, the act of intercourse, and varieties of sexual expression depend to a large extent on the individual's prior history with matters of nudity and sexuality, and the degree of acceptance or rejection he has developed concerning his own sexuality. If he accepts his own sexuality and maintains positive attitudes toward the opposite sex, then erotic stimuli will arouse sexual desire and curiosity for further exploration. Typically, such exploration is rather limited in scope, and the aroused desire is reduced through the adolescent outlet of masturbation.

If an individual has developed feelings of confusion and guilt concerning his sexuality during preadolescence, his reactions to erotica as a teen-ager will mirror this internal conflict. Sexual arousal will elicit guilt and disgust, emotions that will serve to reinforce his sense of distaste regarding his own sexual desires. Even the use of masturbation to relieve sexual tensions fits this cycle, as masturbation too will generate increased guilt. It is not entirely true, however, that reactions to erotica universally elicit negative reactions in these individuals. There are frequent instances in our interviews in which noncontrols reported that the erotic stimulus they found most memorable was the only one encountered in adolescence that portrayed sex as a pleasurable and desirable activity.

Erotica serves not only to arouse sexual desires but also to provide models of sexual behavior. As indicated previously, some of these models relate to the anatomy of the human body and the specifics of sexual relations. In the latter case, the models portray the behavior and attitudes of both sexes. On a behavioral level, erotica is not limited to the culturally sanctioned act of heterosexual intercourse with the man on top, but portrays numerous positions and varieties of sexual relations (oral-genital relations, multiple sex partners, homosexuality, etc.).

The individual's reaction when exposed to these various stimuli apparently relates to his previously established sexual identity, rather than influencing the development of that identity. Since our subjects were rarely exposed to homosexual erotica as adolescents, their reactions to heterosexual erotica are most significant. For the developing heterosexuals, on one hand, these stimuli served an educational function, combining with information garnered from peers to suggest the range of heterosexual practices open to them. The developing homosexuals, on the other hand, focused not on the activity portrayed, but rather on the female's behavior — selecting that aspect of the material congruent with their incipient homosexual identity. These data confirm our earlier conclusion (based on our review of previous studies) that sex role identity is a significant factor in determining response to erotica.

Further confirmation is provided by the finding that most of the homosexuals had already begun experimenting with same-sex relations (one-third by age fourteen) prior to any significant exposure to homosexual erotica. Typically, this kind of erotica was first encountered in late adolescence or early adulthood, when the homosexual's behavior patterns were already established. Homosexuals, then, rarely if ever develop their sexual preference as a result of exposure to homosexual erotica. Rather, their vague adolescent sense of this emerging identity leads them to respond to heterosexual erotica differently from the heterosexually developing male.

A similar relationship between internalized values and response to erotica can be seen for erotica encountered during teen-age years which portrayed aggression toward another as part of the sexual act. With this kind of material, standards and values concerning aggression or debasement of others became the salient factor in determining the emotional reactions of the viewer. Most of our subjects, as adolescents, reacted to erotica depicting subtle or obvious sadism with feelings of disgust and rejection.

Social scientists, in attempting to evaluate the impact of symbolic behavior models during formative years, have usually tried to isolate the existing data into one of three models: an *arousal* model, an *imitation* model, and a *catharsis* model. In the case of the first, symbolic media act to intensify one's motivation to act in a particular way, but the overt behavior that follows will be dependent upon one's past history, ego controls, and inner values. The second model assumes that attractive and powerful models will be imitated on a covert and overt level. The third assumes that vicarious participation in a process of emotional arousal (a fight scene in a movie, for example) drains off psychic tensions by reducing the level of motivation. Thus, people who view a fight scene in a movie should be less angry, less likely to fight upon provocation than a group not so exposed. In most of this theorizing, it is not always clear whether the focus is on short-term or long-term effects of exposure to symbolic media, as one can experience catharsis in the short run while subconsciously absorbing patterns of aggressive behavior which may influence one's actions at a later date.

What do our data indicate concerning each of these models? First and foremost, they suggest that it is very difficult to consider a particular model as existing independently of the others. During formative years, erotica clearly arouses sexual interest and drive. The behavior induced by this erotica is very much dependent upon the individual's previously developed sex role identity, the extent of his guilt feelings about sex (if any), and the level of his self-control. In general, little *overt* imitation of behavior displayed in erotica is noted. Considerable *covert* imitation occurs in the form of fantasies — mental images of the opposite sex and sexual relations in general — which serve to nurture an emerging sexual curiosity. When the individual is older, he may attempt overt imitation of those practices described in the erotica that conform to his personal set of standards and values. Thus, there appears to be a "network censor" that screens the variety of images garnered from erotica and permits overt imitation only of those activities congruent with one's self-concept, view of the opposite sex, and general ethical values. This selective imitation enables the adolescent to "try on" his heterosexual role and learn what sexual practices give him satisfaction.

There are also suggestions that exposure to erotica during adolescence serves a cathartic function. Sexual tensions are often reduced through masturbatory activity, a useful short-term technique. Erotica does not serve as the major source of arousal leading to masturbatory activity, but rather as one of the set of sexual stimuli to which the teen-ager reacts. Real people in his environment are far more potent sexual stimuli. The cycle of arousal and sexual release through masturbation appears to have the long-range effect of generating continued interest and curiosity about actual heterosexual contacts.

Our data indicate reasonably clearly that the arousal theory and the imitation theory possess limited validity in explaining the impact of symbolic representations of sexuality upon the developing adolescent male. The catharsis theory applies only when we consider the cycle of arousal and release through self-stimulation. Each of these theories covers some portion of our findings, but none seems sufficiently complete to cover the full range of short- and long-term reactions to erotica. Arousal theory best fits the short-run reactions and imitation theory the long-range effects, if the latter theory is modified to include the concept of a filtering agent which selects acceptable models for subsequent imitation.

It is not surprising that erotica seems to serve different functions for the adult than it did for the adolescent. For example, adults rarely learn anything new about sexual behavior from erotica, although they may see graphic representations of behavior they had only read about as adolescents. Sexual identities and patterns are ordinarily well established by adulthood, and there is little likelihood that imitation of new sexual practices will be attempted. Generally, erotica affects adults significantly only in that it increases their interest in sex and arouses their sexual impulses. The behavior it stimulates is likely to be a repetition of their regular sexual activity rather than some novel behavior (J. Mann, et al., 1970). The impact of erotica on adults is very short-lived, typically dissipated in less than a day, and we see much less evidence of long-term preoccupation with the images or themes it presents. In most heterosexual males, an exciting erotic stimulus (this varies with sexual attitudes and values, well established in adulthood) will provide a momentary boost to the sexual drive, increasing the likelihood of sexual activity if a regular sex partner is available.

The relationship between sexual arousal and sexual behavior in the nonheterosexual or sex offender is not so clear-cut, however. There is little, if any, evidence in our data to suggest that exposure to erotica tends to touch off antisocial sexual behavior. In fact, the high degree of sex guilt found in sex offender subject as adults (arousal coupled with disgust and revulsion) seems to inhibit overt imitation of the behavior symbolically portrayed. Most sex offenders appeared to carry through the pattern of arousal and masturbation, so generally characteristic of adolescent males, into their adult lives. Erotica for them becomes a regular stimulus for masturbation, but not for other forms of overt sexual behavior. This normally developing male, by contrast, readily substituted real women for symbolic women and intercourse for masturbation. The utilization of erotica by adult sex offenders represents but one element of a fixated, immature pattern of sexual development. The poor occupational and interpersonal adjustment of most sexual offenders indicates that this sexual immaturity reflects a generally limited social development. Erotica, then, does not seem to be a major stimulus for antisocial sexual behavior in the potential sex offender. In fact, there is some evidence (see chap. 10) that for rapists, exposure to erotica portraying "normal" heterosexual relations can serve to ward off antisocial sexual impulses.

The data collected and analyzed in our study is of a preliminary nature, and all the issues we have discussed certainly merit investigation. Nevertheless, our analysis is congruent with the findings of some forty other studies performed for the Commission on Obscenity and Pornography and supports these conclusions of the Commission:

> The Commission believes that much of the "problem" regarding materials which depict explicit sexual activity stems from the inability or reluctance of people in our society to be open and direct in dealing with sexual matters. This most often manifests itself in the inhibition of talking openly and directly about sex. Professionals use highly technical language when they discuss sex; others of us escape by using euphemisms — or by not talking about sex at all. Direct and open conversation about sex between parent and child is too rare in our society.
>
> Failure to talk openly and directly about sex has several consequences. It overemphasizes sex, gives it a magical nonnatural quality, making it more attractive and fascinating. It diverts the expression of sexual interest out of more legitimate channels, into less legitimate channels. Such failure makes teaching children and adolescents to become fully and adequately functioning sexual adults a more difficult task. And it clogs legitimate channels for transmitting sexual information and forces people to use clandestine and unreliable sources.
>
> The Commission believes that interest in sex is normal, healthy, good. Interest in sex begins very early in life and continues throughout the life cycle

although the strength of this interest varies from stage to stage. With the onset of puberty, physiological and hormonal changes occur which both quicken interest and make the individual more responsive to sexual interest. The individual needs information about sex in order to understand himself, place his new experiences in a proper context, and cope with his new feelings.

The basic institutions of marriage and the family are built in our society primarily on sexual attraction, love, and sexual expression. These institutions can function successfully only to the extent that they have a healthy base. Thus the very foundation of our society rests upon healthy sexual attitudes grounded in appropriate and accurate sexual information.

Sexual information is so important and so necessary that if people cannot obtain it openly and directly from legitimate sources and through accurate and legitimate channels, they will seek it through whatever channels and sources are available. Clandestine sources may not only be inaccurate but may also be distorted and provide a warped context.

The Commission believes that accurate, appropriate sex information provided openly and directly through legitimate channels and from reliable sources in healthy context can compete successfully with potentially distorted, warped, inaccurate, and unreliable information from clandestine, illegitimate sources; and it believes that the attitudes and orientations toward sex produced by the open communication of appropriate sex information from reliable sources through legitimate channels will be normal and healthy, providing a solid foundation for the basic institutions of our society.

It may be that, in a kind of inverse Gresham's Law, good sex education will drive the pornographer out of business. Yet, the difficulties enlightened educators have experienced in attempting to implement some form of approved sex education through public institutions in this country makes it very unlikely that we will see this devaluation of pornography come to pass in the near future. Regrettably, it will probably continue for some time to serve as the primary source of sex education for many young people, particularly those reared in homes where open discussion and information about sex are unavailable.

*I deplore the putrid state
into which our newspapers have passed,
and the malignity, the vulgarity and mendacious spirit of those who write
them. . . . These ordures are rapidly depraving the public taste.
It is however an evil for which there is no remedy,
our liberty depends on the freedom of the press,
and that cannot be limited
without being lost.*

THOMAS JEFFERSON

PORNOGRAPHY AND OBSCENITY:
ITS DEFINITION AND CONTROL
IN A FREE SOCIETY

SCOPE

This work has been concerned with the reporting of data relating to the social and behavioral impact of exposure to erotica. In this concluding chapter, consideration is given to the nature of the potential utilization of the research data in the hands of our lawmakers, including legislators, judges, and the executive branch. It is their function to establish the legal limits, if any, on private and public use and dissemination of pornography. Since much research remains to be done on the behavioral consequences of exposure to erotica, including further intensive analysis of our own data, we do not attempt to draw definitive legal conclusions. Instead, we briefly review the legal history of censorship in this country, commencing with our inheritance from the English system; and then attempt to demonstrate how and why further legal judgments in this area are in large part determined by, and dependent on, the factual realities of social behavior.

A FREE SOCIETY — THE COMMON LAW HERITAGE

The current concern regarding censorship of pornography is not a recent phenomenon, but dates back to the early days of mass communication. Jefferson's eloquent plea for freedom of the press, quoted above, came at a time when that concept was still a relatively new one. Democratic revolutions and social libertarian movements throughout Europe (and subsequently in the New World) had first gained impetus with the invention of the printing press a few hundred years earlier. Reaction to both the social movements and their new tools of pamphlets, newspapers, books, and other writings was not long in coming.

By the seventeenth century, formal systems of censorship had already begun to take root. In England the Royal Prerogative (a collection of rights enjoyed by the king alone, as distinct from all his subjects), was deemed to include the power to grant licenses to print any book or pamphlet. This power over communication was vested by the crown in the court of the Star Chamber, that part of the king's Privy Council that dealt with purely legal questions. This court, which freely utilized torture as a means of investigation and punishment, was completely subservient to the will of the king and effectively controlled on his behalf the free expression of ideas and opinions. Approval in writing from the Star Chamber was required before any material could be printed. This restriction was set up for two purposes: (1) To prohibit the printing of heretical books in opposition to the Church (established by the state and effectively part of the "government"); and (2) to prevent the publication of seditious books directly in opposition to the government.

The Act of 1633, the first act of Parliament relating to the subject, was also directed at those writings the authorities considered seditious or heretical, but this act revised the centers of control. Instead of maintaining the jurisdiction of the Court of the Star Chamber over all works, the act divided responsibility among several authorities, according to subject matter. For example, political works came under the authority of the secretary of state, and law books under the lord chancellor. General works were placed under the ecclesiastic authority of the archbishop of Canterbury and the bishop of London, thus establishing an early and direct relationship between religious and moral acceptability and the right to publish.

The Act of 1633 was allowed to expire in 1695. After 1696 there was no specific law governing what might be printed, though there still remained the general English laws that provided severe punishments for the crimes of sedition and blasphemy. Cases concerning pornography and obscenity, apparently not yet major issues, were handled by the ecclesiastic courts.

A case in point arose in 1663, when Sir Charles Sedley relieved his bladder while standing above the crowd on the balcony of Covent Garden, and thereafter threw bottles at the bystanders who gathered below. The urinating and self-exposure were considered doubtful offenses, and punishment followed only because the bottle-throwing constituted a breach of the peace, punishable in the regular courts. In 1708 the case against an open and prolific pornographer was dismissed, the court stating that there was no law to punish this offense, as it was not a libel of any person but rather a general offense against morals — a matter for the ecclesiastic courts (*Regina v. Read,* Fortescue 98 [1703]).

It was not until a series of cases beginning with *Regina v. Curll* (Cobbitt, vol. 17 [1727]) that pornography and obscenity as such became punishable under the common law. Bearing in mind the conviction of Sir Charles, who threw bottles as well as simply exposing himself, and the acquittal of Read, who did not openly breach the peace but merely printed words, the attorney general in *Regina v. Curll* argued for a new rule of law in these matters. He urged that the peace can be breached without actual force and by words alone, if the words constitute an act against the constitution, civil government, religion, or morality.

As to morality. Destroying the peace of the government; for government is no more than public order which is morality. My Lord chief justice Holt used to say, Christianity is part of the law; and why not morality too?

Curll was convicted, with the court treading the semantic path from pornography to immorality to heresy to illegality.

A FREE SOCIETY — NATIVE ORIGINS

Curll was convicted less than fifty years before England felt the reverberations from the shot fired at Concord Bridge heralding the birth of a new nation. Midwives present included such wielders of the pen as Tom Paine, a dedicated agitator and atheist. The appearance of his major work, *The Age of Reason,* in England resulted in the conviction of its publisher for blasphemous libel. Paine had attacked the Old Testament as a brutalizing and corrupting influence on mankind. The new nation was to separate church from state, a political decision made under the influence of "blasphemers" such as Paine as well as those strongly religious persons who feared the Old World's restrictions on freedom of worship. The laws of the mother country punished not only those who rejected all religion but also those whose religious views differed from those of the established church.

The leaders of the new nation, whose existence was ushered in by seditious writings such as the Declaration of Independence and blasphemies such as Paine's, whose population consisted largely of persons who had fled or whose parents had fled various forms of restraint on liberty and open expression of belief and opinion, faced the task of writing a constitution that would protect the freedom so avidly sought.

The ratification of the United States Constitution occurred only after the adoption of the Bill of Rights, with its firm guarantee of both freedom of speech and freedom of religion. In view of the then recently decided *Curll* case, wherein religious belief was used as the justification for restriction of freedom of speech, the first amendment juxtaposition of those freedoms was a curious one indeed, and to this day there remains the possibility of conflict when the strictures of that amendment are applied to cases involving pornography and obscenity. This possibility of conflict between two protected values is not the result of poor draftsmanship or inadequate conceptualization, but is inherent in the nature of constitutional democracy.

A "pure" democracy, one with absolute majority rule, would have no use for a Bill of Rights or many other aspects of the Constitution — any more than would a monarchy or dictatorship. As amended, the Constitution creates a limited democracy, a constitutional democracy, one that guarantees to minorities — even a minority of one — certain rights and privileges, including the right to make known to others and to urge upon them one's ethical, political, and religious views, no matter how unpopular, antiestablishment, or contrary to the views of the majority they may be.

It is only under this form of government that the question of control of pornography and obscenity becomes a debatable issue. In a government that does not guarantee freedom of speech, the ruling authority need only decide what it deems to be pornographic or obscene and prohibit it.

A FREE SOCIETY — MODERN AMERICA

Free Speech. Are speech and other forms of expression entirely unbridled in a democratic society? Some of our constitutional scholars, and some judges, have maintained that all ideas may be openly expressed, and no restraints can be placed upon them in the name of obscenity or pornography. See, for example, the dissenting opinions of Justices Black and Douglas in *Roth v. U.S.,* 354 U.S. 476 (1957) and their separate opinion in *Jacobellis v. Ohio,* 378 U.S. 184 (1964). This view is not now and probably never has been the controlling majority view of our courts.

Legal commentators and judges in the past and at present have found it appropriate to justify constitutional limitations on speech not expressing a point of view or a religious tenet. The classic illustration is that provided by Justice Holmes: "The most stringent protection of free speech would not protect a man in falsely shouting fire in a theatre, and causing a panic" (*Schenck v. United States,* 249 U.S. 47 [1919]).

In some cases, speech that does express a particular point of view may present legal problems. Seditious speech, suggesting actions that constitute a clear and present danger to others, has been held criminal (*Schenck v. United States*). The "clear and present danger" test helps to distinguish that speech which represents an expression of belief from that which is a call to action (*Abrams v. United States,* 250 U.S. 616 [1919]). It is clear, nevertheless, that the seemingly absolute protection of speech by the First Amendment is not now and never has been held to be absolute by our highest judicial body. But limits have only been imposed on freedom of speech where the social or political values being protected are deemed of the most compelling nature and of the highest order, such as the preservation of national security or the prevention of violent crimes.

In making any decision regarding such limitations, as in making any constitutional judgment, the Supreme Court must balance different and frequently conflicting social and political policies and values. If the court gives too much weight to the alleged political or social danger, real or imaginary, citizens will become reluctant to speak out on current issues. If it appears to interpret the First Amendment as offering carte blanche to writers, speakers, publishers, and so on, it will hear the indignant outcries of those whose beliefs or values have been attacked or ridiculed in the offending material.

Nothing in the Constitution expressly gives to the Supreme Court the right to determine whether particular laws or actions are constitutional. This power is considered a necessary implication of its duty to decide cases while sworn to uphold the Constitution (*Marbury v. Madison,* 1 Cranch 137 [1803]). If a law or action violates a constitutional restraint, then that law or action must be curtailed. Every lawmaker, prosecutor, law enforcement official, and state and federal judge, is also sworn to uphold federal and state constitutions, and they should neither enact nor enforce laws, nor take any action, they know to be unconstitutional.

Because upholding the United States Constitution and its amendments requires a constant balancing of conflicting social and political policies and values, it is not surprising that in many important areas the rules undergo continual change. Until very recently, the basic legal definition of "obscene" in this country was derived from the case of *Regina v. Hicklin,* L.R. 3, Q.B. 360 (1868), which established this test: ". . . whether the tendency of the matter charged as obscenity is to deprave and corrupt those whose minds are open to such immoral influences, and into whose hands a publication of this sort may fall."

What is perhaps most interesting about that case, which established the definition of obscenity both in England and the United States for almost one hundred years, is that it centered on the conflict between protection of speech and protection of religion, and the latter prevailed. The pamphlet involved in *Regina v. Hicklin* was an anti-Roman Catholic tract entitled "The Confessional Unmasked." It purported to reveal the depravity of the priesthood, and included some remarks on the type of questions put to females in the confessional. It was clear in that case that the pamphlet was not written for prurient purposes but as a source of information, in that its immediate object was not to deprave the public mind but to destroy Roman Catholicism. Nevertheless the work was banned and its creators found guilty of purveying obscenity to the public.

The *Regina v. Hicklin* definition was essentially unchanged until *Roth v. United States,* supra (1957), which defined obscene material as that in which the dominant theme appeals to the prurient interest of the average person, applying contemporary community standards. Under this test, the tract censored in *Regina v. Hicklin* undoubtedly would not have been prohibited.

Since *Roth v. United States,* the Supreme Court and other major state and federal courts in the United States have issued a continuing series of conflicting and frequently incomprehensible opinions dealing with censorship. This judicial production has been accompanied by alternate cries of joy and anguish from opposing factions of the public — all perfectly consistent with our form of government. One of this country's most honored judges, Benjamin Nathan Cardozo, put it this way in *The Paradoxes of Legal Science* (1928):

> Logic and history and custom and utility and the accepted standards of right conduct are the forces which singly or in combination shape the progress of the law. Which of these forces shall dominate in any case must depend largely upon the comparative importance or value of the social interests that will thereby be promoted or impaired.

One premise on which our constitutional democracy is based is that the responsibility for evaluating the importance of these "social interests" in a particular case must be assigned to the disinterested judiciary, rather than the public at large. The validity of this premise is illustrated by a recent newspaper story reporting that, of fifty persons asked to sign a statement — which, unknown to them, was a reprint of the Bill of Rights — forty-nine refused and the fiftieth requested a dollar in exchange for his signature. None of the fifty recognized the document, and many assailed the petitioner for treason and sedition.

An eloquent expression of the dangers inherent in any restriction of the right to free speech is contained in the following statement, part of

Thomas Erskine's defense of a publisher charged with libeling the House of Commons:

> From minds thus subdued by the terror of punishment there could issue no works of genius to expand the empire of human reason, nor any masterly compositions on the general nature of government by the help of which the great commonwealth of mankind have founded their establishments. Under such terrors all the great lights of science and civilization must be extinguished; for men cannot communicate their free thought to one another with a lash held over their heads.

Erskine's argument illustrates the paradox that is crucial to any examination of censorship: trends of thought that one generation may consider seditious, obscene, and/or heretical are often recognized as the "great lights of . . . civilization" by the next. Not long ago, such topics as contraception, abortion, and sex education were mentioned in hushed whispers, if at all. Yet these issues are now the focus of widespread social and scientific study, and developments in all three areas are highlighted regularly in the daily papers. This kind of shift in public tolerance has long been acknowledged as a natural aspect of the evolution of human society, in the words of Justice Holmes in his dissenting opinion in *Abrams v. United States,* "[T]ime has upset many fighting faiths." Holmes elaborated on this premise in the same opinion:

> The ultimate good desired is better reached by free trade in ideas — [the] best test of truth is the power of thought to get itself accepted in the competition of the market. . . . That at any rate is the theory of our Constitution. It is an experiment, as all life is an experiment. Every year if not every day we have to wager our salvation upon some prophecy based upon imperfect knowledge. While that experiment is part of our system I think that we should be eternally vigilant against attempts to check the expression of opinions that we loathe and believe to be fraught with death, unless they so imminently threaten immediate interference with the lawful and pressing purposes of the law that an immediate check is required to save the country.

THE ASSUMPTIONS OF THE CURRENT LAW

'Twas brillig, and the slithy toves
   Did gyre and gimble in the wabe:
All mimsy were the borogoves,
   And the mome raths outgrabe.

LEWIS CARROLL,
Through the Looking Glass

In *Roth v. United States,* the definition of prurient material that could be censored came alongside the restriction that censorship would not be allowed if the material had some socially redeeming significance. In that opinion, the Court assumed that prurient interest per se is bad — bad enough to deprive the prurient work of constitutional protection, unless the material as a whole could be said to have some social merit.

If prurient materials are "bad" only as measured by an "ideal" or abstract moral or religious standard but do not lead to the commission of antisocial or criminal acts, why is it required that this class of material must have a compensating ingredient of socially redeeming significance to be permitted? Ratner has observed (1969) "That kind of material has traditionally been subjected to community regulation, although such regulation intrudes upon the privacy of personal thoughts, inhibits the exchange of sexual ideas, and probably reflects, in a significant part, a 'quasi religious' view of erotic fantasy as sinful." Ratner attacks the "utterly without redeeming social importance" concept of obscenity as invalid, because it reflects a particular judicial attitude toward sex. Why withdraw the First Amendment protection if the material presents no clear and present danger, regardless of whatever social importance it may or may not have? Why is sex singled out for this special treatment?

The research reported in this work clearly tends to support the view that pornography does not incite criminal or antisocial acts. Indeed, some of the data suggest the reverse may be true; greater and earlier exposure to erotic material might have been educational and lessened the development of antisocial and deviant attitudes and behavior in certain persons so disposed. If our data are valid, and if further studies verify our conclusions, is there any justification in imposing the special requirement of "socially redeeming purpose" for this class of materials? Why is redemption required if there is no legal or demonstrated social evil for which compensation is necessary. By way of contrast, there is no requirement of socially redeeming purpose in publications of a nonsexual nature involving violence, sadism, or other socially unacceptable elements.

Part of the answer undoubtedly is directly traceable to the politico-religious development of censorship laws previously discussed. In part, the special treatment accorded to sexual materials has more indirect religious and moral overtones such as is found in the attitudes of those procensorship writers whose disapproval of pornography seems to stem from their view that masturbation is inherently bad. Lockhart*

---

* William B. Lockhart, as a consequence of serving as the chairman of the United States Commission on Obscenity and Pornography and thereby becoming familiar with the social and psychological facts uncovered through the work of the Commission, so changed his views with regard to the censorship of pornography that he joined in the conclusions of the Commission. As set forth at the end of chapter 11, these conclusions indicate a dramatic shift in the views of Professor Lockhart on the effects of pornography and the need for openness in discussing erotic and sex-related materials.

and McClure (1961) label pornography as repulsive material, intended primarily to nourish erotic fantasies and encourage autoeroticism, and Benjamin Karpman (1954) labels it a form of "psychic masturbation." Ratner disagrees, holding that sexual gratification is a basic human need satisfied in many different ways, and techniques that satisfy that need perform an important function.

The Supreme Court indicated recognition of this position in *Stanley v. Georgia,* 394 U.S. 557 (1969), stating that a person is entitled to possess pornography in the privacy of his own home; that the Constitution protects the right to receive information and ideas, regardless of their social worth; and that one may satisfy his intellectual and emotional needs in the privacy of his own home by the use of pornographic materials, if so desired.

With regard to the argument that pornography and obscenity create a clear and present danger to the public welfare, and that censorship is required to reduce "deviant sexual behavior or crimes of sexual violence," the Court made its most cogent pronouncement. After reviewing materials summarizing the present state of knowledge on the alleged causal connections between obscenity and antisocial behavior (including part of the data presented in this report), the Court observed in *Stanley*:

There appears to be little empirical basis for establishing such a connection. . . . The Court may no more prohibit mere possession of obscenity on the ground that it may lead to anti-social conduct than it may prohibit possession of chemistry books on the ground that they may lead to manufacture of homemade spirits.

This evaluation by the U.S. Supreme Court of the available empirical evidence concerning the possible causal nexus between obscene materials and antisocial conduct has just been completely turned about in three decisions, all announced on June 21, 1973, as this work was going to press. In *Kaplan v. California,* No. 71-1422 and in *Paris Adult Theatre I v. Slaton,* No. 71-1051, the Court expressed views that can be interpreted to mean: (1) each State may assume that there is a direct causal connection between obscenity and antisocial conduct because the relationship is inherently unprovable (and thus not disprovable); or (2) each State may assume such a relationship because it has not as of this date been disproved. On either theory, each State may constitutionally adopt limits on commerce in obscenity.

In *Kaplan* the Court stated:

A State could reasonably regard the "hard core" conduct described by *Suite 69* as capable of encouraging or causing antisocial behavior, especially in its impact on young people. States need not wait until behavioral experts or educators can provide empirical data before enacting controls of commerce in obscene materials unprotected by the First Amendment or by a constitutional right to privacy. We have noted the power of a legislative body to enact such regulatory laws on the basis of unprovable assumptions.

In *Paris Adult Theatre I* the Court expressly responded to the argument that commerce in obscene materials could not be restricted because of the lack of demonstrated adverse affects as follows:

But, it is argued, there is no scientific data which conclusively demonstrates that exposure to obscene materials adversely affects men and women or their society. It is urged on behalf of the petitioner that absent such a demonstration, any kind of State regulation is "impermissible." We reject this argument. It is not for us to resolve empirical uncertainties underlying state legislation, save in the exceptional case where that legislation plainly impinges upon rights protected by the Constitution itself. MR. JUSTICE BRENNAN, speaking for the Court in *Ginsberg v. New York,* 390 U.S. 629, 643 (1968), said "We do not demand of legislatures 'scientifically certain criteria of legislation.' *Noble State Bank v. Haskell,* 219 U.S. 104, 110." Although there is no conclusive proof of a connection between antisocial behavior and obscene material, the legislature of Georgia could quite reasonably determine that such a connection does or might exist. In deciding *Roth,* this Court implicitly accepted that a legislature could legitimately act on such a conclusion to protect *"the social interest in order and morality. . . ."*

"From the beginning of civilized societies, legislators and judges have acted on various unprovable assumptions. Such assumptions underly much lawful state regulation of commercial and business affairs. . . ." If we accept the unprovable assumption that a complete education requires certain books . . . and the well nigh universal beliefs that good books, plays, and art lift the spirit, improve the mind, enrich the human personality and develop character, can we then say that a state legislature may not act on the corollary assumption that commerce in obscene books, or public exhibitions focused on obscene conduct, have a tendency to exert a corrupting and debasing impact leading to antisocial behavior? "Many of these affects may be intangible and indistinct, but they are nonetheless real. . . ." The sum of experience including that of the past two decades, affords an ample basis for legislatures to conclude that a sensitive, key relationship of human existence, central to family life, community welfare, and the development of human personality, can be debased and distorted by crass commercial exploitation of sex. Nothing in the Constitution prohibits a State from reaching such a conclusion and acting on it legislatively simply because there is no conclusive evidence or empirical data.

In the third case decided the same day, *Miller v. California,* No. 70-73, the Court appears to have substituted for the *Roth* standard of lack of redeeming social value a new standard that the work, taken as a whole, must lack serious literary, artistic, political, or scientific merit. The Court further expressly confined the permissible scope of such a requirement to works that depict or describe sexual conduct. (Was the Court's failure expressly to include scatological materials — recall Sir Charles who relieved his badder above the crowd at Covent Garden — an oversight, an enlightened view, or an immature judgment of the scope of sexual conduct?) As in the past, the Court has made no attempt to indicate why such a requirement of "redemption" or "merit" is required for sexually explicit materials as distinguished from materials of an aggressive or violent or "worthless" nature. As Justice Douglas stated in his dissent in *Miller*: "As is intimated by the Court's opinion, the materials before us may be garbage. But so is much of what is said in political campaigns, in the daily press, on TV or over the radio."

These excerpts from the *Kaplan* and *Paris* decisions are interesting in that in the one case (*Paris*), the Court states that the legislature may assume obscenity leads to antisocial acts, although it has not yet been so proven (implicitly assuming that it will be so proven), and in the other case (*Kaplan*), the Court, in effect, states that such proof is unnecessary since the assumption can be made and it is not subject to test. One frequently hears the facetious statement "Don't confuse me with the facts," but it is to be hoped that this is not the principle now adopted by the highest court in our land.

It has been the purpose of the research reported in this work to try to enlarge the empirical factual base on which judgments can be intelligently and objectively founded concerning the relationship between obscenity and antisocial behavior, and the need, if any, for pornography either to be prohibited or redeemed by the addition of socially ameliorating elements. The available data tend to side with Lewis Carroll:

> "The time has come," the Walrus said,
>   "To talk of many things;
> Of shoes — and ships — and sealing-wax —
>   Of cabbages — and kings —
> And why the sea is boiling hot —
>   And whether pigs have wings."
>   (*Through the Looking Glass*)

CLINICAL RESEARCH INSTRUMENT

STAGE 1: INTRODUCTORY STATEMENT

With the freer expression of sex in public today, as in magazines and movies, we have all had some experience with erotic material in which sex is shown or described openly. Some people find this material interesting and others do not. We are carrying out a research survey to find out what people have seen or read and their reactions. We would like to ask you some questions about your experiences with erotic material. If we are going to find out people's views on this matter, your answers to these questions are important. Of course, there are no "right" or "wrong" answers.

Your answers will not be identified with you in any way. Your responses will be tabulated with those of other people questioned, with no reference to you. The interview will take approximately one hour of your time.

STAGE 2: DEMOGRAPHIC DATA

1. Where were you born?
2. What is your birthdate?
3. Where have you been living for the past year?
4. How many years have you lived in (3)?
5. How large a place is (3)?
   a. large city (population over 1,000,000)
   b. suburb of a large city
   c. medium-sized city (100,000–1,000)
   d. small town
   e. rural or farm area
6. Are you married? (*If "yes," ask questions a–c; if "no," ask question 7.*)
   a. How long have you been married?

    b. How many times have you been married?

    c. How long did each marriage last?

7. Are you divorced, separated or widowed? (*If "yes," ask questions a–c.*)

    a. How long have you been divorced (separated) (widowed)?

    b. How many times have you been married?

    c. How long did each marriage last?

8. Do you have any children? (*If "yes," ask questions a–c.*)

    a. How many?

    b. What are their ages?

    c. Are they boys or girls?

9. How far did you go in school?

    a. less than eighth grade

    b. eighth grade

    c. some high school

    d. high school graduate

    e. some college (freshman, sophomore, junior, senior)

    f. college graduate

    g. some graduate work (no degree)

    h. graduate degree (M.A., Ph.D.)

    i. professional degree (M.D., lawyer, etc.)

10. What do you do for a living?

11. How many different jobs have you had within the past five years?

12. What is the best job you ever had (the one you liked the best)? What was your salary?

13. How do you feel about your current job? (If unemployed, ask about last job.)

    a. satisfied

    b. all right, but would like to change

    c. boring

    d. unsatisfied

14. (*Ask only if respondent is bored or unsatisfied with current job.*) What about your job bores you or is unsatisfying?

15. How do you feel about the salary you are earning in your present (or last) job?

    a. satisfied

    b. unsatisfied

16. What is your average yearly income? (If married, include spouse's income.)

17. What religion were you raised in? (Probe for denomination.)

    a. Protestant

    b. Roman Catholic

    c. Jewish

  d. atheist, agnostic

  e. other

18. What church do you now belong to, if any?

  a. Jewish

  b. Protestant

  c. Roman Catholic

  d. atheist, agnostic

  e. other

  f. none

19. How often have you gone to church or church-sponsored activities during this year?

  a. once a week or more

  b. several times a month

  c. about once a month

  d. several times a year

  e. about once a year or less

  f. not at all

STAGE 3: PREADOLESCENCE, ADOLESCENCE, AND RECENT
EXPERIENCE WITH EROTIC MATERIAL

A. GENERAL

20. Which magazines do you read regularly?

21. About how often do you go to the movies?

22. How often do you go out and see live entertainment in theaters or in nightclubs or bars?

23. Tell me what you have seen or read within the past year in which nudity or sex acts were shown or described.

24. Could you tell me what was shown or described?

25. (*Ask if no response to 23.*) Well, for example, tell me about any scenes that you have seen in movies recently, in which nudity and sexual acts were portrayed.

26. Often when kids are growing up, that is in their preadolescent period (anywhere between 6, 7, 8, 9, and 10), they come across materials in which nude people are shown or described. What did you come across?

27. What was it?

28. (*Ask 28 and 29 if no response to 26.*) For example, did any kids or grownups ever show you a book, cartoons, or pictures of nude people?

29. Who showed it to you?

30. Where were you?

31. Who were you with?
32. When was the first time you saw ————?
33. What did you learn from ————?
34. Did you learn anything about sex from ————?
35. (*If "yes" to 34.*) What was it?
36. Was there anything you found out about sex that you later learned was not so?
37. (*If "yes" to 36.*) What was it?
38. Did you do anything of a sexual nature after seeing ————?
39. Would you have liked to?
40. How about materials in which sex acts were shown or described?
41. (*Ask 41–48 if "yes" to 40.*) Where were you when you saw ————?
42. When was the first time you saw ————?
43. What did you learn from ————?
44. What did you learn about sex from ————?
45. Was there anything you found out about sex that you later learned was not so?
46. (*If "yes" to 45.*) What was it?
47. Did you do anything of a sexual nature after seeing ————?
48. Would you have liked to?

B. SPECIFIC EROTIC SCENES, ADOLESCENCE

Photographs

> (*If a "yes" response is given to any
> of the following questions, ask:*
> How many   have you seen?*)

49. Now, thinking about your adolescent period, do you remember having seen photographs, drawings, cartoons of nude women?
50. What about photographs of nude women showing their sex organs?
51. What about photographs of nude males?
52. What about photographs of nude males showing their sex organs?
53. How about pictures of sexual intercourse?
54. What about photographs of couples in mouth-genital contact?
55. How about photographs in which people were shown to whip, spank or force each other to do something, or other similar activities?
56. How about pictures of homosexual acts (or lesbian acts)?
57. Any other kind of photographs that we have not covered?
58. Generally, how did you come across these pictures?

Movies

> (*If a "yes" response is given to any of the
> following questions, ask:*
> a. How many _____ have you seen?
> b. What were their names?
> c. Was that a commercial or private film?)

59. Now, let us talk about movies that you saw in your teens. Do you remember having seen movies in which there were nude women?
60. How much nudity was shown?
61. What about nude males?
62. How much nudity was shown?
63. What about movies in which sexual intercourse was shown?
64. How about movies in which couples were shown in mouth-genital contact?
65. How about homosexual activity (or lesbian activity)?
66. What about movies in which people were shown to whip, spank or force each other to do something or similar activities?
67. Any other kind of movies that we have not covered?
68. Generally, how did you come across these films?

Books

> (*If a "yes" response is given to any of the follow-
> ing questions, ask:*
> a. How many _____ did you come across?
> b. What was their name?)

69. Now let us talk about the books you have read in your teens. Have you read any books in which nudity or sexual acts of any type were described?
70. How about books describing sexual intercourse?
71. How about books describing homosexual acts (or lesbian acts)?
72. Books in which people were described as having mouth-genital contact?
73. How about books describing people whipping or spanking or forcing each other to do something, or similar activities?
74. How about any other sexual scenes described which we did not cover?
75. Generally, how did you come across these books?

C. INTENSIVE QUESTIONS FOR ADOLESCENCE

76. Of all these photographs, films and books that you have mentioned seeing during your teens, which really stands out in your mind the

most? (*If no response:* If I were to say the word "erotic" what would be the first thing that comes to your mind?)

77. What about _____ makes it stand out in your mind so strongly?
78. Could you tell me what was shown or described?
79. Where did you see it?
80. Were you using alcohol, pot or other stuff at the time?
81. (*Ask 81 and 82 if "yes" to 80.*) When? (before, during, after)
82. Which one? In what way did this affect your reaction to _____?
83. What about it was sexually exciting?
84. People often have more than one reaction, both pleasant and unpleasant. What were your other feelings?
85. Did anything about it disgust you?
86. (*If "yes" to 85.*) What was it?
87. What about it made you angry?
88. What about it shocked you?
89. How old were you when you saw it?
90. Who was with you at that time? (Probe for males and/or females; how many of each.)
91. (*If other people present, ask 91–93.*) Whose idea was it to see or read _____?
92. What was their reaction?
93. In what way did their reaction affect you?
94. a. Was there anything about sex in _____ that you had never heard of before?
    b. Was there anything in _____ that you had never seen before?
95. Did you understand what was going on?
96. (*Ask 96–98 if "no" to 95.*) Who did you ask for some information, if anyone?
97. What kind of an answer did you get?
98. Did you believe what you were told?
99. What about sex did you learn from _____?
100. Was there anything you found out about sex from _____ that later in life you learned was not so?
101. (*If "yes" to 100.*) What was it?
102. Did you think about it later?
103. Was there anything shown or described in _____ that you wished you could later try? (New techniques, new ways of having sex: oral-genital, many partners.)
104. What was it?

105. Did you try it?
106. (*If "no" to 105.*) What prevented you from doing it?
107. (*If "yes" to 105.*) How did you feel afterward?
    If subject does not report having engaged in sexual activity to 103, then ask 108
108. (*If "no" to 103.*) What kind of sexual activity did you feel like engaging in after seeing _____?
109. Did you do it?
110. (*If "no" to 109.*) What prevented you from doing it?
111. (*If "yes" to 109.*) How did you feel afterward?
112. How often have you seen _____ like this during your teens?
113. Most people after seeing _____ of this kind want to obtain some of their own, were you able to find your own?
114. (*Ask 114–116 if "yes" to 113.*) How did you obtain it?
115. How many?
116. How often did you look at or read _____?
117. Every kid thinks about sex and daydreams about it. How often did you think about sex during your teens?
    a. almost never
    b. good part of the time
    c. always
118. In what ways did scenes from these movies, books or photographs come to be a part of your daydreams or thoughts? Would any specific scenes come to mind while daydreaming?
119. We know from Kinsey and similar studies that almost all kids masturbate during their teens. How often did thinking or daydreaming about any of these materials excite you to masturbate?
120. (*If subject reports masturbation, ask 120.*) Did you usually masturbate while looking at the material or just thinking about it?
121. Of all these pictures, films and books that you have seen during your teens, which one did you find the most sexually exciting?
122. Could you tell me why?
123. Which one did you find the most disgusting?
124. Why?
125. During your teens, in addition to these photographs, films and books, what other things usually turned you on? (You know, like clothing or objects of same or opposite sex.)
126. When was the first time you became aware of this kind of excitement?
127. How did you try to repeat this experience?

D. SPECIFIC EROTIC SCENES, RECENT EXPERIENCE

Photographs

> *(If a "yes" response is given to any of the*
> *following questions, ask:*
> How many _____ have you seen?)

128. Now, let us talk about your recent experience, let us say within the past year. Have you seen photographs, drawings, cartoons of nude women?
129. How about nude women in which their sex organs are revealed?
130. What about pictures of nude males?
131. How about nude males in which their sex organs are revealed?
132. What about pictures of sexual intercourse?
133. How about pictures of homosexual activity (or lesbian activity)?
134. What about pictures of couples in mouth-genital contact?
135. How about pictures in which people were shown to whip, spank or force each other to do something?
136. Any other kind of pictures about sex which we did not cover?
137. Generally, how did you come across these pictures? (Probe for where.)

Movies

> *(If a "yes" response is given to any of the*
> *following questions, ask:*
> a. How many _____ have you seen?
> b. What was their name?
> c. Was it a commercial or private film?)

138. Within the past year, have you seen movies in which nude women appear?
139. How much nudity was shown?
140. What about movies in which nude men appeared?
141. How much nudity was shown?
142. How about movies in which sexual intercourse was shown?
143. Have you seen movies in which homosexual activity (or lesbian activity) was shown?
144. What about movies of couples in which mouth-genital contact was shown?
145. How about movies in which people were shown to whip, spank or force each other to do something, or similar activities?
146. Any other kind of movies which we did not cover?
147. Generally, how did you come across these films?

Books

> (*If a "yes" response is given to any of the*
> *following questions, ask:*
> a. How many _____ have you read?
> b. What were their names?)

148. During the past year have you read any books in which nudity or sexual acts of any type was described?
149. What about books describing homosexual activity (or lesbian activity)?
150. How about books describing sexual intercourse in detail?
151. What about books in which people were described as having mouth-genital contact?
152. How about books in which people were described as spanking, whipping or similar activities?
153. Any other books describing sexual activities which we have not described?
154. Generally, how did you come across these books?

Live Shows

> (*If a "yes" response is given to any of the*
> *following questions, ask:*
> a. How many _____ have you seen?
> b. Was this a private or public show?)

155. Within the past year have you seen live entertainment with topless women?
156. How about belly dancers?
157. Live shows in which women appeared completely nude?
158. What about shows of homosexual activities (or lesbian activities)?
159. How about shows in which sexual intercourse was shown?
160. What about shows in which people engaged in mouth-genital contact?
161. How about shows in which people engaged in whipping or spanking or similar activities?
162. Any other kind of live entertainment which we have not covered?
163. Generally, how did you come across shows like this?

E. INTENSIVE QUESTIONS FOR RECENT EXPERIENCE

164. Of all these photographs, movies, books and live shows that you have seen within the past year, which really stands out in your mind the most? (*If no response:* How about in recent years? *If no response:* How about in your lifetime? *If no response:* If I were

to say the word "erotic" what would be the first thing that comes to your mind?)

165. What about _____ makes it stand out in your mind so strongly? (Probe for specific scenes.)

166. Could you tell me what was shown or described? Which scene or episode particularly stands out in your mind? What makes it stand out?

167. Where did you see it?

168. Were you using alcohol, pot or other stuff at the time?

169. (*Ask 169 and 170 if "yes" to 168.*) When? (before, during, after)

170. Which one? In what way did this affect your reaction to _____?

171. a. Was there anything in what you saw that you had not heard of before?
    b. Was there anything you hadn't seen before?

172. (*If "yes" to 171 a or b.*) What was it?

173. What about sex did you learn from this?

174. Was there anything shown or described in _____ that you wished you could later try? (New techniques, new ways of having sex, etc.)

175. (*If "yes" to 174, ask 175–178.*) What was it?

176. Did you later try it?

177. (*If "no" to 176.*) What prevented you from doing it?

178. (*If "yes" to 176.*) How did you feel afterwards?

179. (*If "no" to 174, ask 179–182.*) What kind of sexual activity did you feel like engaging in after seeing _____?

180. Did you do it?

181. (*If "no" to 180.*) What prevented you from doing it?

182. (*If "yes" to 180.*) How did you feel afterwards?

183. What about _____ was sexually exciting, you know, really turned you on?

184. As we mentioned before, people often have more than one reaction, both pleasant and unpleasant. What were your other feelings?

185. Did anything in _____ disgust you?

186. (*If "yes" to 185.*) What was it?

187. What about it made you angry?

188. What about it shocked you?

189. How often have you seen _____ like this recently?

190. As we said before, most people after seeing _____ like this want to acquire some for their own use. Did you want to obtain some for yourself?

191. (*If "yes" to 190.*) Were you able to obtain any?

192. (*If "yes" to 191.*) How did you get it?

193. (*Ask 193 and 194 if "yes" to 192.*) How many _____ do you have?
194. How often do you look at it?
195. Who were you with when you saw _____?
196. (*If other people present, ask 196–198.*) Whose idea was it to see _____?
197. What was their reaction?
198. In what way did their reaction affect you?
199. People usually think and daydream about sex. How often do you find your thoughts or daydreams drifting around topics of sex?
200. What parts or scenes from _____ appeared in your daydreams?
201. How do you feel when these thoughts reappear in your mind?
202. During the past year, how often did thinking or daydreaming about any of these sexual materials which we have discussed excite you to masturbate?
203. (*If subject reports masturbation, ask 203.*) Did you usually masturbate while looking at the material or just thinking about it?
204. How frequently would you masturbate when not thinking about these materials? What were you thinking about?
205. Did these thoughts excite you to have sexual relations? How often?
206. (*If "yes" to 205.*) What kind of sexual activity did you engage in? (homosexual, heterosexual)
207. (*If "yes" to 205.*) How often were these thoughts present during your sexual activity?
208. Of all these pictures, films, books, and live shows that you have seen recently, which one did you find the most sexually exciting?
209. Could you tell me why?
210. Which one did you find the most disgusting?
211. Could you tell me why?
212. In addition to these materials, what other things have usually turned you on recently (such as clothing or objects pertaining to the same or opposite sex)?
213. When was the first time you became aware of this kind of excitement?
214. In what ways did you try to repeat this experience?
215. Do you own any erotic material?
216. (*If "yes" to 215.*) Could you tell me what you own (pictures, books, films) and how many of each?

F. THE ROLE OF FANTASY

Now let us talk more generally about imagination and its role in sex. Most people find it more exciting to have daydreams or fantasies about sex. You know, thinking about sexual experiences that have happened or making up experiences that have not happened. Some people find it exciting to daydream about these things before having sex and others like to continue imagining throughout the sex act.

217. Are your sex fantasies or daydreams always pretty much the same or do they vary? (*If subject reports no fantasy, ask 232. If response is still negative, proceed to 228.*)
218. Do you have sex fantasies when you are alone? What is happening in the fantasy?
219. Do you have sex fantasies during the sex act?
220. In your fantasies do you think about your sex partner or some other person?
221. Could you tell me what's happening in the fantasy?
222. Are you one of the persons involved?
223. What are you doing?
224. What else is going on in your imagination?
225. Who else is in the fantasy?
226. Do you find daydreaming more exciting during the sex act or before?
227. How often do you daydream during sex acts?
228. As part of your current sexual life, in what ways do you use books, pictures, films, or other materials to arouse yourself?
229. In what way do you use these for the purpose of arousing your partner? Does your partner use these to arouse you?
230. In what way does this help to sexually stimulate your partner?
231. How about yourself?
232. Do you ever have fantasies about:
    a. heterosexual intercourse with your partner
    b. oral-genital activity
    c. homosexual acts
    d. whipping and spanking or forcing people to do something they don't want to do
    e. being whipped or spanked or being forced to do something you don't want to do
    f. being dressed in clothing of other sex
    g. how about sex with a person other than the person that you are making it with
    h. sex involving many different people (orgies)
    i. animals
    If a "yes" response is given to any of the above, ask:
    j. Did you come across this idea in any erotic material?
    k. How old were you when you started having this fantasy?
233. (*If "yes" to 217 or 232.*) To what extent have you been able to

find books, pictures or films which vividly portrayed your favorite sexual daydreams?

234. Have you learned any new sex techniques from the erotic materials you have seen?

235. Have these erotic materials had any effect on your attitudes toward sex?

236. Do you feel that you enjoy sex more as a result of the erotic materials you have seen?

237. Do you think that your experience with erotic materials has increased the frequency of your sexual activity?

238. If you had Aladdin's Lamp and the Genie could create the most arousing erotic material for you, what would you ask him to create?

239. Do you regard these erotic materials that you have seen or read as being what people actually do or are they just a figment of somebody's wild imagination?

240. Which ones are real and which ones are not?

STAGE 4: PARENTAL AND SUBJECT SEX ATTITUDES

Now I would like to ask you some general questions about your background. For most of these questions I'll give you a card and ask you to read the answer you choose.

A. PARENTAL SEX ATTITUDES

241. What was the attitude toward nudity in your home when you were a child? When you were a teenager?
    a. very casual, much nudity
    b. casual, some nudity
    c. concerned that people were properly covered
    d. very concerned, no nudity

242. How often was sex the subject of general family conversation?
    a. frequently
    b. occasionally
    c. seldom
    d. never

243. What kind of erotic materal was available to you around the house? Did your parents know you saw it? What was their reaction?

244. How often would you say your parents attended religious services or church-sponsored activities?
    a. once a week or more
    b. several times a month

    c. about once a month

    d. several times a year

    e. about once a year or less

    f. not at all

245. Which of the following have given you a good deal of information about sex, and when was this?

	good deal	some	little	none at all	age at the time
a. father					
b. mother					
c. brothers					
d. sisters					
e. other relatives					
f. male friends					
g. female friends					
h. teachers					
i. clergymen					
j. doctors					
k. reading on your own					
l. sex education course in school					
m. wife					
n. husband					

246. When did you have a course in school in which you received any sex education?

    a. junior high school

    b. high school

    c. college

    d. never

247. (*If had sex education in school, ask 247–249.*) Was the material presented in the course new to you or you already knew most of it?

248. Did you learn anything about the act of sexual intercourse?

249. Did the course contain any instruction about birth control methods?

B. SUBJECT SEX ATTITUDES

250. How comfortable do you generally feel when talking about sex?

    a. comfortable

    b. somewhat comfortable

    c. somewhat uncomfortable

    d. uncomfortable

    e. never talk about it

251. Who do you think should have access to explicit manuals of sexual intercourse?
    a. anyone
    b. anyone over 21
    c. anyone over 18
    d. anyone over 13
    e. only married couples or those about to be married
    f. no one
252. What about materials in which nudity or sex acts are shown or described?
    a. anyone
    b. anyone over 21
    c. anyone over 18
    d. no one
253. What do you think is the best source of sex education for girls? Boys?
    a. books
    b. friends
    c. school
    d. parents
    e. church
    f. other (please specify)
254. What is your opinion about homosexuality?
    a. There is nothing wrong with it; there is an element of homosexuality in everyone.
    b. It is a character disorder, a kind of mental illness, and homosexuals need therapy.
    c. It is a perversion and should be suppressed.
255. What do you think of prostitution?
    a. It is a matter of individual choice, and should be legalized with some degree of governmental control.
    b. It is a character disorder, some kind of sickness, and prostitutes need therapy.
    c. It is a perversion and should be suppressed.
256. How do you feel about premarital sexual intercourse?
    a. It is all right for both young people and adults.
    b. It is all right for consenting adults.
    c. It is all right for couples who share affection.
    d. It is all right for couples who are in love.
    e. It is all right for couples who are engaged.
    f. It is wrong; couples should wait until they are married.
257. What would you feel to be an appropriate standard of sexual behavior?

a. Men and women should be free to decide for themselves about premarital and extramarital sexual intercourse.

b. Men and women should be free to engage in premarital intercourse, but not extramarital.

c. Women should not agree to extramarital intercourse, but it is reasonable to expect that men will.

d. Premarital relations are permissible for either sex.

e. Women should not engage in either premarital or extramarital intercourse, but men may.

f. Men, but not women, may engage in premarital intercourse; neither men nor women should have extramarital intercourse.

g. Neither men nor women should have sexual relations outside of marriage.

STAGE 5: SEX HISTORY AND CURRENT SEX PRACTICES

A. SEX HISTORY

258. How old were you at the time of your first heterosexual intercourse?
   a. 14 or younger
   b. 15–17
   c. 18–20
   d. 21–23
   e. 24–28
   f. 29–33
   g. 34–38
   h. 39–older
   i. none

259. With whom was your first intercourse?
   a. spouse after marriage
   b. fiancé or fiancée
   c. steady date
   d. someone you had known for a while but not dated steadily
   e. casual acquaintance
   f. stranger
   g. prostitute
   h. relative
   i. none

260. With how many persons have you had premarital sexual intercourse?
   a. none
   b. 1
   c. 2
   d. 3

     e. 4

     f. 5

     g. 6

     h. 7 or more

261. Have you ever been married? If so, with how many different persons have you had extramarital sexual intercourse?

     a. none

     b. 1

     c. 2

     d. 3

     e. 4

     f. 5

     g. 6

     h. 7 or more

     i. never married

262. How old were you at the time of your first masturbation?

     a. 5 or younger

     b. 6

     c. 7

     d. 8

     e. 9

     f. 10

     g. 11

     h. 12

     i. 13

     j. 14

     k. 15

     l. 16

     m. 17

     n. 18 and over

     o. never

263. How did you find out about masturbation?

     a. told by a friend (same age)

     b. told by a friend (older)

     c. parents

     d. books

     e. formal sex education in high school or college

     f. observed a friend (same age)

     g. observed a friend (older)

     h. observed a stranger

B. CURRENT SEX PRACTICES

264. Do you have a steady sex partner?

265. Do you have more than one?
266. (*If "yes" to 265.*) How many during the past year?
267. Are these partner(s) of the opposite sex?
268. (*If "no" to 267.*) Are these partners of the same sex?
269. Have you attended an orgy recently?
270. How often do you have sexual intercourse each week, on the average?
    a. 6 or more times a week
    b. 4–5 times a week
    c. 2–3 times a week
    d. once a week
    e. less than once a week
271. In what ways do you achieve or help your partner to achieve orgasm, other than intercourse?
    a. light petting (deep kissing and breast touching)
    b. heavy petting (touching sex organs)
    c. mouth-genital relations
    d. anal intercourse
    e. other
272. Which of the following describes your experience of sexual intercourse?
    a. very enjoyable
    b. neither pleasant nor unpleasant
    c. very unpleasant

STAGE 6: CONCLUSION

273. How do you feel about the fact that sexual matters are expressed more freely and openly in public these days?
274. Do you feel that people could get hurt by seeing movies of pictures or books about sexual acts?
275. How do you feel about kids seeing these kinds of materials?
276. Do you feel there should be laws regulating what people see and read?

Appendix Table 1

AGE DISTRIBUTION

| | | | Atascadero Samples | | | | | Blacks | |
Age Group	Control	Rapist	Male Object Pedophile	Female Object Pedophile	Homosexual	Transsexual	Users	Ghetto	Mid-class
15-19	5.7	5.3	10.0	0.0	2.7	15.4	5.6	9.1	0.0
20-24	43.4	36.8	10.0	15.0	8.1	15.4	18.2	45.5	5.9
25-29	30.2	21.1	30.0	10.0	21.6	30.8	30.2	13.6	23.5
30-34	9.4	21.1	15.0	20.0	18.9	38.5	11.7	22.7	35.3
35-39	7.5	10.5	10.0	40.0	8.1	0.0	4.3	4.5	17.6
40-44	0.0	5.3	20.0	0.0	16.2	0.0	18.2	0.0	11.8
45-49	1.9	0.0	0.0	5.0	5.4	0.0	8.0	4.5	5.9
50-59	1.9	0.0	0.0	0.0	13.5	0.0	3.7	0.0	0.0
60-	0.0	0.0	5.0	10.0	5.4	0.0	0.0	0.0	0.0
N	53	20	20	20	37	13	78	22	17
vs. controls	—	—	.05	.01	.01	—	.05	—	.01

Appendix Table 2
MARITAL STATUS

	Atascadero Samples						Blacks	
Status	Control	Rapist	Male Object Pedophile	Female Object Pedophile	Homo-sexual	Trans-sexual	Users	Ghetto	Mid-class
Married	41.5	42.1	30.0	55.0	2.7	15.4	33.4	40.9	47.1
Separated	5.7	15.8	0.0	10.0	0.0	7.7	6.3	0.0	5.9
Divorced	5.7	15.8	10.0	25.0	16.2	15.4	13.4	13.6	17.6
Widowed	0.0	0.0	5.0	0.0	0.0	0.0	0.6	0.0	0.0
Single	45.3	21.1	55.0	10.0	70.3	61.5	45.0	40.9	23.5
N	53	20	20	20	37	13	78	22	17
vs. control	—	—	—	.01	.01	—	—	—	—

Appendix Table 3

EDUCATION

	Atascadero Samples							Blacks	
Education	Control	Rapist	Male Object Pedophile	Female Object Pedophile	Homo-sexual	Trans-sexual	Users	Ghetto	Mid-class
Less than 8th	1.9	0.0	15.0	5.0	0.0	0.0	0.0	4.5	0.0
8th	3.8	0.0	5.0	10.0	2.7	0.0	0.0	4.5	5.9
Some H.S.	15.1	42.1	35.0	50.0	2.7	30.8	8.9	45.5	23.5
H.S. grad.	30.2	31.6	15.0	30.0	16.2	15.4	18.6	36.4	11.8
Some college	41.5	26.3	20.0	5.0	43.2	15.4	43.1	9.1	29.4
College grad.	3.8	0.0	5.0	0.0	10.8	7.7	11.5	0.0	11.8
Some grad.	1.9	0.0	0.0	0.0	10.8	15.4	6.9	0.0	11.8
Grad. degree	2.9	0.0	5.0	0.0	10.8	15.4	7.8	0.0	5.9
Prof. degree	0.0	0.0	0.0	0.0	2.7	0.0	1.3	0.0	0.0
N	53	20	20	20	37	13	78	22	17
vs. controls	—	—	—	.01	.01	.02	.01	.02	—

Appendix Table 4

EDWARDS OCCUPATIONAL SCALE OF SOCIOECONOMIC STATUS

Occupation	Atascadero Samples							Blacks	
	Control	Rapist	Male Object Pedophile	Female Object Pedophile	Homo-sexual	Trans-sexual	Users	Ghetto	Mid-class
Maj. prof.	0.0	0.0	5.0	0.0	10.8	7.7	15.4	0.0	0.0
Lesser prof.	1.9	0.0	5.0	0.0	18.9	23.1	7.6	0.0	29.4
Minor prof.	5.7	0.0	5.0	5.0	5.4	7.7	17.9	4.5	11.8
Clerical	22.6	10.5	0.0	10.0	21.6	0.0	13.4	0.0	5.9
Skilled man.	26.4	26.3	20.0	15.0	5.4	7.7	3.9	4.5	17.6
Semiskilled	5.7	42.1	35.0	45.0	2.7	7.7	5.2	9.1	11.8
Unskilled	15.1	10.5	15.0	20.0	10.8	0.0	6.9	4.5	0.0
Unemployed	17.0	5.3	5.0	5.0	16.2	23.1	16.3	13.6	5.9
Student	5.7	0.0	0.0	0.0	2.7	7.7	10.8	59.1	11.8
N	53	20	20	20	37	13	78	22	17
vs. controls	—	.01	.01	.01	.01	.01	.02	.01	.01

REFERENCES

Abelson, H.; Cohen, R.; Heaton, E., and Suder, C. 1970. "Public attitudes toward and experience with erotic materials." Technical reports of the Commission on Obscenity and Pornography, vol. 6. Washington, D.C.: U.S. Government Printing Office.

Athanasiou, R., and Shaver, P. 1969. "A research questionnaire on sex." *Psychology Today* (July): 64–69.

Bandura, A.; Ross, D.; and Ross, S. A. 1961. "Transmission of aggression through imitation of aggressive models." *Journal of Abnormal and Social Psychology* 63: 575–582.

Bell, A. P., and Hall, C. S. 1971. *The personality of a child molester.* Chicago: Aldine-Atherton.

Benjamin, H. 1953. "Transvestism and Transsexualism." *International Journal of Sexology* 7: 12–14.

Berkowitz, L., and Rawlings, E. 1963. "Effects of film violence on inhibitions against subsequent aggression." *Journal of Abnormal and Social Psychology* 66: 405–412.

Clark, R. A. 1952. "The projective measurement of experimentally induced levels of sexual motivation." *Journal of Experimental Psychology* 44: 391–399.

Coleman, J. C. 1972. *Abnormal psychology and modern life.* 4th ed. Chicago: Scott-Foresman & Co.

Feshbach, S. 1961. "The stimulating versus cathartic effect of a vicarious aggressive activity." *Journal of Abnormal and Social Psychology* 63: 381–385.

———, and Singer, R. D. 1971. *Television and aggression.* San Francisco: Jossey-Bass.

Freud, S. 1907. "Creative writers and daydreaming." In vol. 9 of *The Writings of Sigmund Freud,* pp. 141–153. London: Hogarth.

Frisbie, L. 1969. "Another look at sex offenders in California." California State Department of Mental Hygiene.

Gebhard, P. H.; Gagnon, J. H.; Pomeroy, W. B., and Christenson, C. V. 1965. *Sex offenders: an analysis of types.* New York: Harper & Row.

Gillette, P. P. "A study of rapists." 1971. Undergraduate honors thesis, University of California at Los Angeles.

Goldberg, P. A., and Milstein, J. T. 1965. "Perceptual investigations of psychoanalytic theory concerning latent homosexuality in women." *Perceptual and Motor Skills* 21: 645–646.

Goldhirsh, M. I. 1961. "Manifest content of dreams of convicted sex offenders." *Journal of Abnormal Psychology* 63: 643–645.

Hooker, E. G. 1962. "The homosexual community." *Proceedings of the XIVth International Congress of Applied Psychology: Personality Research* 2: 40–59.

"J." 1969. *The Sensuous Woman.* New York: Lyle Stuart.

Jakobovits, L. A. 1965. "Evaluational reactions to erotic literature." *Psychological Reports* 16: 985–994.

Kaplan, A. 1955. "Obscenity as an esthetic category." *Law and Contemporary Problems* 20: 552–559.

Karpman, B. 1954. The sexual offender and his offenses. New York, Julian Press.

Kinsey, A. C.; Pomeroy, W.; and Martin, T. 1948. *Sexual behavior in the human male.* Philadelphia: W. B. Saunders Co.

————. 1953. *Sexual behavior in the human female.* Philadelphia: W. B. Saunders Co.

Kronhausen, E., and Kronhausen, P. 1964. *Pornography and the law.* New York: Ballentine Books.

Leiman, A. H., and Epstein, S. 1961. "Thematic sexual responses as related to sexual drive and guilt." *Journal of Abnormal and Social Psychology* 63: 169–175.

Levitt, E. E. 1969. "Pornography: some new perspectives on an old problem." *The Journal of Sex Research* 5: 247–259.

Levitt, E. E., and Hinesley, R. K. 1967. "Some factors in the valences of erotic visual stimuli." *The Journal of Sex Research* 3: 63–68.

Lindner, H. 1953. "Sexual responsiveness to perceptual tests in a group of sexual offenders." *Journal of Personality* 21: 364–374.

Lockhart, W. B., and McClure, R. C. 1961. "Obscenity censorship: The Core Constitutional Issue—What Is Obscene?" 7 *Utah Law Review* 289.

Loiselle, R. H., and Mollenauer, S. 1965. "Galvanic skin responses to sexual stimuli in a female population." *Journal of Genetic Psychology* 73: 273–275.

Mann, J.; Sidman, J.; and Starr, S. 1970. "Effects of erotic films on sexual behaviors of married couples." Technical reports of the Commission on Obscenity and Pornography, vol. 8. Washington, D.C.: U.S. Government Printing Office.

Miller, D. R., and Swanson, G. E. 1960. *Inner conflict and defense.* New York: Holt, Rinehart & Winston.

Mosher, D. L. 1970. "Psychological reactions to pornographic films." Technical report of the Commission on Obscenity and Pornography, vol. 8. Washington, D.C.: U.S. Government Printing Office.

Mosher, D. L., and Greenberg, I. 1969. "Females' affective responses to reading erotic literature." *Journal of Consulting and Clinical Psychology* 33:472–477.

Mussen, P. H., and Scodel, A. "The effects of sexual stimulation under varying conditions on TAT sexual responsiveness." *Journal of Consulting Psychology* 19: 90.

Polsky, N. 1967. *Hustlers, beats and others.* Chicago: Aldine Publishing Co.

Pomeroy, W. B. 1969. "Transsexualism and sexuality: sexual behavior of pre- and postoperative male transsexuals." In *Transsexualism and sex reassignment,* ed. R. Green and J. Money, pp. 183–188. Baltimore: The Johns Hopkins Press.

Ramsey, G. 1943. "The sexual development of boys." *American Journal of Psychology* 56: 217–233.

Ratner, L. G. 1969. "The Social Importance of Prurient Interest–Obscenity

Regulations v. Thought–Privacy." 42 *Southern California Law Review* 587.

Schmidt, G., and Sigusch, V. 1970. "Psychosexual stimulation by films and slides: a further report on sex differences." *Journal of Sex Research* 6: 10–24.

Schroeder, T. 1954. "Phallic Worship to a Secularized Sex." *Sexology* 20: 481–483.

Singer, J. L. 1966. *Daydreaming.* New York: Random House.

Staub, E., and Konn, L. K. 1970. "Aggression." In *Symptoms of psychopathology: A handbook,* ed. C. G. Costello, pp. 481–510. New York: John Wiley & Sons, Inc.

Stoller, R. J. 1970. "Pornography and perversion." *Archives of General Psychiatry* 22: 490–499.

U.S. Commission Report on Obscenity and Pornography. 1970. Washington, D.C.: U.S. Government Printing Office.

Zamansky, H. S. 1956. "A technique for assessing homosexual tendencies." *Journal of Personality* 24: 436–446.

INDEX